Editorial

The 24 July issue of *Publishers' Weekly* includes reviews of seven poetry titles forthcoming between July and September. They come under the heading 'Review Fiction'. *PW* – the leading trade journal, comparable to the British *Bookseller* – does these features quarterly because an appetite for poetry among booksellers in the United States is assumed to exist.

The books chosen are diverse in many ways. They are all by authors whose work has sold well or been well reviewed in the past. What is striking to see, for a British publisher, is the fact that all but one of the books featured are over 100 pages in extent and priced between $16 and $26 (£12.45 and £20.23). Ben Lerner's *The Lights* is the most expensive, a 128-page 'muted and heartfelt' hardback collection from Farrar, Straus and Giroux. The others are all paperbacks, the most expensive per page being by the best-known of the poets, Terrance Hayes. *So to Speak* is a $20 Penguin weighing in at 112 pages. 'Across three various and virtuosic sections,' *PW* tells its readers, 'Hayes *(American Sonnets for My Past and Future Assassin)* examines the personal and public, from fatherhood to the murder of George Floyd, in his muscular and meditative seventh collection.' It notes how 'Many lines have an aphoristic intensity ("A god who claims to be on the side of good // but remains hidden is strange as the rules of grammar"), providing moments of sharp clarity within longer narratives.' It also notes how 'Hayes reinvents received forms, from the "Do-it-Yourself Sestina" to "A Ghazzalled Sentence After 'My People... Hold On'" by Eddie Kendricks, and the Negro Act of 1740'. 'The assumption is that booksellers want to know about the poems as poetry, not only what they say but how they work and what they do. To read such comments in a trade journal is bracing: text written by an informed reader rather than a marketing department. Other descriptions have a little too much blurby residue about them: 'Wry and invigorating, this resonant collection mollifies the need for certainty.' 'By using the pig as both subject and object, Sax navigates queerness, filth, beauty, and capitalism, exploring at all times "the animal yearning / within the animal within the animal."' 'Finding beauty in the lowest, filthiest things, these poems guide the audience's gaze toward redemption.'

Two of the books featured come from Graywolf Press (Mary Jo Bang's *A Film in Which I Play Everyone* and Sally Wen Mao's *The Kingdom of Surfaces*). Others are published by Scribner, Wesleyan University Press (*Selected Poems of Calvin C. Hernton*, a scholarly re-introduction of the cofounder of the Umbra Poets Workshop and member of the Black Arts Movement, 1932–2001, 'a pioneer in the field of Black studies who placed his contributions and identity as a poet above his other accomplishments'), and Trio House, whose mission is to produce no more or fewer than three new books of poems a year.

PW provides a helpful window into how the American book trade deals with poetry. An *editorial* interest is taken in it, the forward recommendations are informed by commercial considerations and at the same time a wide cultural respect. The list proposed is necessarily selective but none the less diverse, suggestive, indicative.

It is also following the growing opposition by writers to their work being used in AI programming. The grounds of their protest are straightforward: their creative and scholarly work is being appropriated without permission or remuneration. The Authors' Guild, the largest professional organisation of writers, has organised an open letter (with approaching 8,000 signatories) addressed to the heads of OpenAI, Alphabet, Meta, Stability AI and IBM. They should stop using writers' work 'without consent or credit' (*Guardian*, 23 July). Many of the usual righteous suspects have signed, making three key demands: the AI companies should 'Obtain permission for use of our copyrighted material'; 'Compensate writers fairly for the past and ongoing use of our works'; and 'Compensate writers fairly for the use of our works in AI output, whether or not the outputs are infringing under current law'. What is disappointing is that the argument is based entirely on remuneration, and the cultural and political principles underlying the AI appropriations remain unquestioned. 'The Authors Guild is taking an important step to advance the rights of all Americans whose data and words and images are being exploited, for immense profit, without their consent,' said Jonathan Franzen.

This is not the first organised protest. Lawsuits based on copyright law have been started. The Society of Authors in the UK has backed these North American initiatives. Nicola Solomon, chief executive of the Society of Authors, pushes the issues further, but so far the Society has not acted in its own: 'The principles of consent, credit and compensation are bedrocks of our intellectual property regime, and a critical part of every author's ability to protect and make a living from their work,' she declared, but inched beyond the material argument when she added, 'The race to build the next generation of systems is driven primarily by the profit motives of large corporations. It is opaque, unfettered and unregulated, while the ethical ramifications of AI systems are complex and crying out for scrutiny.' It is the ethical ramifications that are likely to be most pertinent in the world of poetry, and these may well go beyond 'establishing safeguards, regulation and compensation'.

Letters to the Editor

Mark Haworth-Booth writes: While I agree with the thrust of Silis McLeod's article on 'The Con of the Wild', [s]he is wrong about Knepp. The rewilding estate is not in 'rural Suffolk' but in Sussex. The remark that Knepp 'is a hybrid between Michael Crichton's Isla Nublar and a very middle-class Butlins' is not convincing. I certainly enjoyed a morning walk around Knepp, a year or two ago, seeing white storks and listening to nightingales. Knepp introduced regenerative farming on the estate in 2021 and deserves credit for that too.

Silis MacLeod replies: I would like to thank Mr Haworth-Booth for putting me right about Sussex. He is also correct that regenerative farming should be commended when and wherever it appears. But large-scale rewilding principles – such as those pursued at Knepp – perpetuate, if not tacitly reward, unsustainable and ultimately unjust models of land ownership. (This may be more apparent in Scotland than across the border.) That the 'estate' is gaining legitimacy in our modern times is a phenomenon about which we should be wary. After all, these estates were the sites of the socially disatrous agricultural 'improvements' in the eighteenth and nineteenth centuries.

News & Notes

Georg-Büchner-Prize awarded to Lutz Seiler • *Evelyn Schlag writes:* The most prestigious prize in German literature has been awarded to a magician of poetic language. Lutz Seiler, born in Gera in the former GDR in 1963, grew up in a little village in Eastern Thuriniga which had to give way to uranium mining when he was five years old. Those industrial landscapes have fed his imagination, both in his poetry and in his two much acclaimed novels about the decline of the GDR. In one of them he described the workings of a poem: 'The good poem must be one big cascade, a glittering streaming in that magic light which it keeps itself reproducing.'

Seiler divides his time between Stockholm and the Peter Huchel House in Wilhelmshort near Berlin, whose keeper he is. In a short essay in 2020 he writes about his forays into the pine tree woods surrounding the house. He is standing under the 'fairy-tale like asymmetries' of their branches, talking and listening to them. He reads in heavy rain (outdoors due to Covid) and the audience orders him to keep reading until everything and everyone is wet to the bone, even the book is dissolving.

A true conjuror, he has rightly joined the company of his great countryman Wolfgang Hilbig, that other bulwark of German poetry and prose.

Gioconda Belli wins Reina Sofia Poetry Prize • The exiled Nicaraguan poet and novelist Gioconda Belli has received this year's Queen Sofia Ibero-American Poetry Prize (the twenty-third). Belli is much loved and widely translated (into twenty languages). She has published novels, essays, children's books and, most notably, fifteen collections of poetry, the first in 1972. The award is the most significant for Spanish and Portuguese poetry. She responded on Twitter, saying 'I dedicate it to my Nicaragua, mother of my inspiration, sorrowful country of my hope'.

Belli was stripped of her Nicaraguan citizenship by the government of President Ortega. She lives in Spain. Like other Ortega critics, her properties in Nicaragua were seized by the government in February. The jury selected her for 'su expresividad creativa, su libertad y valentía poéticas' and also for her significance in contemporary Nicaraguan culture. She prevailed in a field of fifty candidates and is the third Nicaraguan to be thus recognised, after Ernesto Cardenal (2012) and Claribel Alegria (2017).

Joan Margarit Prize for Poetry • Sharon Olds has already won a National Book Critics' Circle Award and a Pulitzer Prize, and the T.S. Eliot Prize in the UK. This award confirms her international following. The prize is administered by the Instituto Cervantes and La Cama Sol publishing house, supported by the family of the poet Joan Margarit (1938–2021).

Catherine Vidler • *Bill Manhire writes:* The Australian poet Catherine Vidler died suddenly on the last day of April, just a few months after her fiftieth birthday. She began writing seriously at the beginning of the century; her first substantial book, *Furious Triangle*, appeared from Puncher & Wattmann in 2011. There was already a procedural element in her work, and this developed in conventional ways (a preoccupation with sestinas, for example) and more adventurously through constraints and collaborations, as well as through lists and digital pattern-making. In recent years she turned more and more to visual work with such projects as her *Chaingrass* poems, *Lost Sonnets*, and *Wings*, these mostly appearing from a range of small publishers, among them SOd Press, Hesterglock Press, Timglaset Editions, Penteract Press, Cordite Books and zimZalla. Most recently, she was making charmingly lyrical images from matchstick arrangements. She often published samples of her wares on Twitter and Instagram, and one way to get a sense of her variousness would be to check **https://twitter.com/usefulstars/media.** Cath also founded and edited the trans-Tasman journal *Snorkel.* Her hope was to reduce the vast awareness gap between Australian and New Zealand writers, a gap that sometimes looks like a bizarre form of sibling rivalry. She herself was an entirely generous writer. She read widely and avidly, and wrote always without rivalry.

Leonard McDermid (1933–2023) • *Robyn Marsack writes*: The death of Len McDermid, after he had enjoyed 'some ninety years of looking at things, and over seventy years of commenting on them in various forms' (as the Scottish Poetry Library has it), marks the passing of a singular life in Scottish poetry, printing and publishing. The esteem and affection with which he was regarded was evident in the shows of 'Fair Wind and Following Seas', curated by Barbara Morton at the Edinburgh College of Art in 2021, and in the expanded version at the SPL in 2022, where his own work was included alongside the tributes from other book artists. For me, it was always a great pleasure to encounter him at the Library, and at the poetry market at StAnza, where he and Jean were regular, benign presences; I am sure I was not the only person who would have liked to buy the entire contents of his Stichill Marigold Press displays.

Born in Kent, Len grew up on Thameside, his father and grandfather having worked in the shipyards at Greenock. He was evacuated to his grandparents' home during the war for a formative year that turned out to include the Clydeside Blitz. An exceptional trio of poets are thus connected: W.S. Graham, born in Greenock in 1918, and Thomas A. Clark, born there in 1944, the sea running through all their work. Len left school at fifteen, and didn't go back to formal education for ten years, when he studied at Medway College of Art, Brighton College of Art, Newbattle in Edinburgh and the University of Edinburgh. He taught art briefly at Aberdeen, then in Edinburgh, and for many years in the Scottish Borders. He went to live in Kelso in 1969, where he had the good fortune to meet and marry Jean; they had two children, Catriona and Finlay. Their home was the appropriately, sunnily named 'Eden Cottage'.

His wasn't a landlocked existence, however. His website recounts that 'In 1984 Len was invited by the Marine Society to work as an art tutor for three months aboard a troopship in the South Atlantic. In 1988 he undertook a further commission at sea, travelling over fifty thousand sea miles to areas including the Americas, Scandinavia, Africa, the Far East, and the Arabian Gulf during the "Tanker War".' One of my favourite pieces is *A Pocket Guide to the Sea*, which I gave to my cousin's son in New Zealand. He is a fisherman and hunter: it gave him joy. He kept it in a special envelope in his pocket, and produced it when men from NZ Fisheries came to bother him with paperwork, to show them what simplicity looked like: 'sail' written in blue on a white page sliced in half diagonally, for example. It is as laconic as the kiwi sense of humour. Greg Thomas, reviewing the SPL show, describes the pleasure of seeing 'an upturned steamer sink[ing] into a blue fabric sea (the front cover of a copy of Henry Newbolt's 1925 text *The Tide of Time*). Its deck, funnel, and hull are embossed with gnomic phrases about to be carried down to Davy Jones's Locker. Then there is the marvellous *Hot Water Tender T42*, an old aluminium kettle decked out with winches, rails, a life-ring and ship's wheel.'

The ship/kettle is the *Earl Grey*, accompanied by a label with a fanciful description of its working life: 'Visual and sculptural symbols are often coaxed into a state of comic or lyrical clarity by annotative notes or poems', Thomas remarks. He is also alert to the context in which Len was working: 'a loosely post-objectivist tradition of minimal nature writing: spartan, speech-paced verse containing traces of folk doggerel and regional demotic. In the 1960s this approach united a group of poets and artists spread between Britain – particularly Scotland – and North America, dubbed "avant-folk" by the critic Ross Hair.'

Of course Ian Hamilton Finlay's work comes to mind as part of this context, but its temper and his temperament are different from what Thomas characterises as the 'generous and ludic assortment' of McDermid's rustic themes: 'seas and rivers, boats and tugs, cornfields and valleys, coal-powered trains, tickets and dockets for the voyage'. Despite their predominance, there is room, too, for a certain sharp wit, as in his late work *Window* (2020), a response to the letterpress project Posted / Unposted British Isles: go to the Stichill Marigold Press's website to see 'A Window on the Political History of Ireland'.

'Marigold' came from the flowers Len and his mother loved, planted from her Gravesend seeds. His pamphlets, prints and cards were all produced using two vintage Adana eight-by-five hand presses and two ten-by-eight Ayers Jardine (Adana) flatbed presses, traditional metal and wooden type, printing blocks and unique hand-cut lino and wood blocks. With typical modesty, he described himself as 'a jobbing artist'. You can see Len's work in the collections of the SPL, the Edinburgh College of Art, the National Poetry Library, Tate Britain and the National Library of Scotland. He won the Callum Macdonald Memorial Award in 2010 (jointly, as publisher for *And For That Minute.*) and in 2018 for his own *Landway*. Part of that award was an appointment as a poet in residence at the Harvard Center for Hellenic Studies Summer School in Nafplio, where he spent an 'amazing' fortnight in 2018. There he found a deep affinity with the Greek poet Stratis Haviaras, his contemporary, who translated some of Len's poems.

I treasure his work for its human scale, its acceptance of imperfections in the hand-making process, its playfulness; for his attentiveness to landscape, seascape and seasonal change, to things that comfort us in this world, from childhood stories to cornfields in the sun. Hardy's 'Afterwards' comes to mind:

> When the Present has latched its postern behind my
> tremulous stay,
> And the May month flaps its glad green leaves
> like wings,
> Delicate-filmed as new-spun silk, will the neighbours
> say,
> 'He was a man who used to notice such things?'

I think they will, and many will miss his gentle, cheerful and perceptive presence. Yet the work remains.

A true homme de lettres • *Raymond Bach writes*: The poet, translator and scholar, David Mus (pen name of David Kuhn) died on 28 May at the age of eighty-seven. His doctoral dissertation for the Sorbonne, 'La poétique de François Villon', was published in 1967 and awarded the Prix Guizot from the Académie Française. Leaving behind a promising academic career in the United States, Mus settled in the small French village of Jailly-les-Moulins, where he devoted himself almost exclusively to the writing and study of poetry. Deeply influenced by his friend and mentor, André du Bouchet, Mus adopted a style in which a complex, often elusive, syntax and inventive typography are counterbalanced by a down-to-earth semantic connection to the daily life of the Burgundian countryside. His works offer us an innovative way of conceiving and representing the intertwining of our physical bodies, our sense of self, the language we use, and the world we inhabit. His earliest publications were in English (e.g., *Wall to Wall Speaks* [Princeton]), but he soon turned to writing bi-lingual French/English collections – *Passion/Passion* (1981) and *D'un accord/Double-stopping* (1991) – in which the two languages dialogue with one another in surprising ways, as well as several remarkable book-length poems in French, including, *Trait sur trait tiré* (1999), *Dehors plutôt qu'ailleurs* (2016) and *Saillie* (2019). A passion for Rome and the ancient world also led him to write on occasion in Italian (*Pagine de giorni senza esito/ Choix de jours sans suite*) and on Italian art (*Tableaux romains*). A complete bibliography can be found in the 2023 issue of *la revue** (*julien nègre, éditeur*), which is devoted to Mus's prose and poetry. David Mus was a true *homme de lettres*, whose work deserves more than the confidential readership it has received until now.

Kickshaws, in memoriam John Crombie •
Peter McCarey writes:

> The moustache said 'I'm grumpy' (which he was)
> though the grey eyes couldn't hide dismay,
> amusement or delight.
> He set up shop in Charité, among funereal florists,
> His printed books – the petals on a lead chrysanthe-
> mum;
> Slept in the back shop – something out of Whitmarsh
> – God knows how.
> Retreated to his pill-box flat in noisy Montparnasse.
> Last time he ventured out on his own, just him and
> his stick,
> A plastic bag for a bottle of J&B,
> A beggar at the bottle shop harassed a man on
> crutches;
> John tried to intervene; the codgers landed in a heap,
> More *Metamorphosis* than his old pal Sam. Which
> made him laugh.

Happy Birthday Ilkley • The Ilkley Literature Festival is celebrating its Jubilee alongside *PN Review*. Only Cheltenham has been going longer. Ilkley runs for seventeen days (6 to 22 October) and has a roster of big-name contributors, though perhaps fewer poets than hitherto. It published some engaging historical facts.

In 1973 J.B. Priestley praised the organisers, noting the difficulty of a literary festival in that, *'Authors have little to show and are no treat as a spectacle.'*

In 1975 his observation was tested. Ted Hughes read *Cave Birds*. The *Yorkshire Post* reported: 'A blood curdling scream pierced the heart of Ted Hughes' new poem sequence at its world premiere in Ilkley… It came from a member of the audience. Shortly afterwards a woman vomited and was led out.'

The national media were excited in 1977 when a huge bronze Minotaur by Michael Ayrton was unveiled for the festival. It sported, as was only proper, *'commensurately large genitalia'*, resulting in petitions to protect the young and the elderly, and a headline in the *Daily Express*, *'Beefing over 7 foot of Bull'.*

An apology • *Michael Schmidt writes: PNR*'s long-standing Subscription Managers and Website Administrators were disappointed and offended by Bill Manhire's 'somewhat flippant' observations regarding the contributors' notes in *PNR*.

His comments were not addressed to the website notes (for which our valued colleagues are consistently responsible, a dedication we value) but to editorial inconsistencies issue by issue – inconsistencies which, alas, go back (on and off) to the earliest days of the magazine and are part of what a generous critic once called its 'settled culture of informality'. Subscribers are urged to visit the website for contributors' notes. Meanwhile, I apologise unreservedly to our digital colleagues, who write: 'The contributor section on the website has been there since its inception. I take a lot of time and effort to keep this up to date, it is a shame that Bill has not taken the time to look.'

Reports

Touch and Mourning

6: Like a Tree in the Forest

ANTHONY VAHNI CAPILDEO

That time in Trinidad when we distilled *Macbeth* into a series of looped, interactive scenes, the play began as soon as you came up the driveway. Someone at a little outdoor table would offer you a stainless-steel bowl to wash your hands in. It had blood-coloured flowers floating in it – the same kind of bowl, in fact it was the same bowl, where raw chicken might be washed with vinegar to remove clots from butchery, and to lighten the meat smell described in Trinidad English as 'fresh'. You would be invited to partake of 'perfumes of Araby', offering you a spritz of some imported cologne. Whatever your gender, whatever your guiltlessness, this introduction makes you complicit. It places you in the role of Lady Macbeth, reimagined as a collective identity, as more people arrive and undergo the ritual welcome.

You enter the play sleepwalking, as a murderess tormented by having the blood of a king on her hands. Mourning and guilt, gilt, gilding, the hands shiny with aromatic oils or bodily fluids, the hands as pages of a state chronicle bound with gold foil, are twinned as fingers scrub and palm wrings out. In the living room, the host does not welcome you. The host is reading aloud the entire play text, softly, continuously, as if they had been 'put so' or 'bewitched' – as if having command of the text were the same as being compelled and zombified – as if the only time we have is the time inside the play. A pine branch hangs suspended from the central ceiling lamp. The living room is the stage and also the forest.

Whatever else Lady Macbeth is doing, she is mourning a version of herself that no ritual can bring into existence again. The violent laying of hands on the royal person, who in Shakespeare's time would have been understood perhaps to have the divine power of healing scrofula by the laying on of hands, is not only profoundly anti-life; it is rehearsed in every gesture that Lady Macbeth will make, ever afterwards, because her hands now gesture as the hands of someone invested with power, someone who has claimed to succeed to power but in fact has seized power and will continue to kill as much as necessary to grasp it. Yet it is not the realm and its people, it is Lady Macbeth she mourns for; like Gerard Manley Hopkins's little girl Margaret, grieving unleaving, but a Margaret all grown up, all fallen.

There is no escaping the forest. Despite wildfires and deforestation, that sense of pure panic which being in a forest can induce – unfolded by Kenneth Grahame, queered by E.M. Forster, embraced by Wilson Harris – stirs in us in 'forest-like' environments, too. Expectations of forest, however, may differ. The feeling of entanglement, the risk of falling into a pit, the lack or patterning of light, the multiplicity of sounds from many directions and sources, the lateral or horizontal brushing or ripping or springing of things against the moving human body, are different in, say, virgin rain forest from in a managed pine wood.

In Shakespeare's play, the third apparition foretells that Macbeth will be undefeated until Birnam Wood comes to Dunsinane. Macbeth, who would like to specialize in wiping out lineages – destroying family trees – imagines trees uprooting themselves to move against him. Knowing himself to be the king of human cutting-down, he sneers:

> Who can impress the forest, bid the tree
> Unfix his earth-bound root?
> (*Macbeth* IV:i)

Although he asks the apparition about any threat from 'Banquo's issue', his boast is that he himself is 'high-placed' and anticipates living 'the lease of nature', a full lifetime.

If you have visited Birnam Wood or anywhere nearby, you will know that the trees in that area are exceptionally tall. No matter their slenderness, their height makes them formidable. To walk among such trees is to see your companions reduced down to another woodland species. This wood belongs to the trees. To think you see such trees marching towards you is not to see nature rising up against you. It is to be made little. The trees hardly have to do anything. Of course, in the play, it is warriors holding trees, to give the illusion of a wood on the move and greater numbers of fighters, at a human level; but the point of the image is that the threat is not at a human level. What Macbeth is closest to touching, compared to such trees, is not the sky – not the supervisory seat of lordship or godly looking-down of kingship. Compared to Birnam Wood, Macbeth is low down, a thing of earth, close to the place of burial, the subterranean banquet-hall of worms. The threat is that the trees will ground him, eternally. A famous man expects a tomb, and public ceremonies of mourning. Macbeth's panic fear is, or should be, for his heroic afterlife. Vain warriors are fine with dying; less so with being lost unlamented. They may touch the living however they like, even to kill them; but mourning that really matters, no mere private grief, is one of their demands.

Moving a little further north, the All-High, the All-Seeing, are titles of the Norse god Óðinn. An oathbreaking, sanity-shattering deity, he takes part in human battles, turning his spear against his devotees, claiming them for death and ultimately himself. He has command of a physical location from which to inspect the three worlds. Macbeth would have loved such a position, and it might have brought him more peace of mind, or greater madness. Imaging armed warriors as forest trees is commonplace in Old Norse literature. The potential of mourning to lead to bodily actions, indeed to violent encounter – mourning as part of power play – is actualized in this tradition. Lament is linked to oath-making, which translates into conflict, and more lament: 'whetting' is the stylized provocation by a woman whose speech acts deliberately swing grief towards anger, inciting others to swear to avenge her loss.

In 'Gerðit hon... sem konor aðrar: Women and Subversion in Old Norse Poetry', an article published in Carolyne Larrington and Paul Acker's excellent volume, *Revisiting the Poetic Edda* (Routledge, 2013), Jóhanna Katrín Friðriksdóttir notes how, in the Eddaic poem *Guðrúnarkviða I*, the heroine Guðrun, when young in sorrow, envisages herself as a small leaf, defined by family and romantic love. Friðriksdóttir contrasts this with another poem, *Hamðismál*, set at a later stage of the cycle of violence. Here, the older and more bereft Guðrun reflects on how many of her kindred have perished. She likens herself to a solitary aspen tree, whereas her family have been broken off like branches from a fir tree. Friðriksdóttir reads this as the expression of a 'sorrow-weary woman and an independent matriarch' – no longer a leaf, but a 'full-grown tree'.

What I see, however, is the aspen tree quivering. It is pale and uncompanioned. It visibly registers every breath of wind. Is it that mourning which fuels power grabs leads to loneliness? Is that where to finish? Or is it with the touch of the invisible made visible? Guðrun's image is not often quoted to its end: she imagines a warm day in the future when a wood-gatherer will come looking for firewood. What a strange – or rather, what a natural, extension of imagery: the humanity of the speaker and her family are composted into the background, and we look forward to what most basically sustains life.

Astropoetics 2

Still in the Snug

DUNCAN MACKAY

It's hard to believe that a decade has passed since our small gathering of astronomers and physicists with an interest in matters literary first met at the local snug here in Canterbury (*PN Review* 214). Participants come and go with the financial and political tides that wash over university life year by year. The pandemic was difficult, of course, and Brexit (while apparently declared a failure) still succeeds in preventing our former flow of enthusiastic students back and forth across *La Manche*, to the detriment of younger generations on both sides. With the concurrent failure of the present government to support UK membership of the Horizon research funding programme, spirits can understandably flag.

In our moments of particular angst, we try to follow the down-to-planet-surface Daoist-cum-Zen advice of one of our long-time favourite poets, Gary Snyder. We have been celebrating his ninety-third birthday (8 May) in recent weeks, by reading from his selected poems collection, *No Nature* (Pantheon, 1992). In his elegy for fellow poet and friend Lew Welch, who disappeared in 1971 and is assumed to have committed suicide (although his body was never found), Snyder expresses the fact of life's continuance in the face of events with the superficially simple but deeply difficult recognition that 'life continues in the kitchen' (from 'For Lew Welch in a Snowfall').

Snyder's phrase has become our mantra as we look beyond to the stars. On the subject of which, three of us have just co-authored an academic text (*Case Studies in Star Formation: A Molecular Astronomy Perspective*, Cambridge UP, 2023) in which we offer an epigraph from the Italian physicist Carlo Rovelli: 'Science is not reliable because it provides certainty. It is reliable because it provides us with the best answers we have at present.' Science, of course, adopts a 'truth-only' criterion by which to judge its best available answers. In contrast, what has been called 'poetic knowledge' seems rather a category of experience, in fact experience experienced through the exploratory process of writing and reading, whose self-justification alone is experience (including that which is beyond reason or beyond words) as an addition to the knowledge pool. Our current challenge is to accept that notion within truth-only criteria.

The 'father of empiricism' is Francis Bacon, whose 'Baconian Method' (the application of inductive reasoning in which generalizations are drawn from abundant evidence) provided the blueprint for the seventeenth-century establishment of 'the' scientific method. Bacon expressed his own insight into this question of balancing analytical objectivity with subjectively experiential knowledge in his work *Novum Organum* (1620). He said: 'experience has not yet become literate', and added: 'No adequate inquiry can be made without writing, and only when that comes into use and experience learns to read and write can we hope for improvement'. Beyond the obvious call for reason over superstition here, the notion of experience learning to read and write seems to us to be almost a description of what Language writers such as Lyn Hejinian have been trying to do. Indeed, Bacon's assertion could almost have been written by Hejinian in an interesting book of her essays that came our way recently, called *The Language of Inquiry*. In it, she writes: 'Poetry comes to know the things that are. But this is not knowledge in the strictest sense, it is, rather, acknowledgment – and that constitutes a sort of unknowing. To know *that* things are is not to know *what* they are, and to know *that* without *what* is to know otherness (i.e., the unknown and perhaps unknowable). Poetry undertakes acknowledgment as a preservation of otherness... The language of poetry is a language of inquiry... It is that language in which a writer (or a reader) both perceives and is conscious of the perception.' Holding that thought, one of our number also recently discovered the British-American writer and critic Elizabeth Sewell (1919–2001): Cambridge graduate, research fellow at Manchester University and long-time academic at several universities in the United States. Sewell appeared to us in the form of a tattered copy, signed by the author, of a collection of her essays at the back of a local charity shop (*To Be a True Poem*, 1979). In one of these essays, Sewell notes that in an address to the 'Reader as Friend', Samuel Taylor Coleridge wrote of the adventure of reading as a search for 'not yet an Other World... but... the other World that now is'. Merging the words that Coleridge himself put in emphasis, Sewell refocused the phrase as 'an other world that now is' in order to emphasize Coleridge's meaning. She pointed out that by splitting the word *another*, Coleridge was reminding us of the many mental constructs that human imaginations have conjured, together constituting any conjectured cumulative knowledge base for understanding 'now'. The point is that neither one definitive model exists nor indeed the duality of two that the familiar use of 'the other' might suggest. 'This or that' may be the usual dichotomy of debate, but therein lies the familiar bifurcation of options that more often than not constrains where a spectrum of possibilities actually exists in reality.

Understanding alternative ways of thinking to our familiar scientific frame of reference became one of the initial motivations for the snug gatherings a decade ago. Of the cumulative knowledge base of human experience to which Sewell refers, there is a simplistic but commonly held view which new members to our group often bring with them, but with which we hope they don't leave. That is the view that even within a strictly rational frame, the arts explore and express individual experience, while the sciences explore and express the collective. Extending that conversation to the notion of 'poetic knowledge' as a contributor to the totality of human knowledge, we recognise that one can also easily misrepresent arts and sciences as exclusively subjective against objective, irrationality against rationality, illogic against logic. Even within a rational frame, Sewell recommends that we consider both 'a rationality and an other rationality'. In other words, she encourages us to accept the spectrum of reasoned but diverse possible conceptual frames that span both the personal and the collective in human experience. Newcomers to our conversations quickly realise that the past one hundred years have seen radically different ways of writing the poetic record of human experience while, perhaps, new ways of reading have yet entirely to catch up. Without getting overly bogged down beyond the simple sensory and intellectual pleasures of reading our favourite writers, that 'how' of how we might read the more nuanced or complex of poetic texts, let alone examples across the spectrum of diverse logics rational or otherwise, has also been part of our snug conversations over the years.

Sewell offers a simple assertion regarding poetry's capacity to prompt for multiple forms of insight and understanding in encompassing our cumulative knowledge across the range of human experience. She says simply that poetry is '*the* most inclusive form of thought we have yet devised'. So where are we so far in our truth-only evaluation of this statement? Rovelli's assertion identifies a distinction between knowledge and truth: there will be things we think we know today that will merit modification in the future in order to qualify as factual truth. Equally, in Hejinian's words, to know *that* is to have knowledge (at least as acknowledgement), while without knowing *what* is to have at best an approximation to what might become subsequent factual truth. Recognising that we all live within a knowledge base filled with the best approximations to the truth available at present seems to us to validate the notion of a collective experientially-derived 'poetic knowledge' (acknowledgement) among poetry's writers and readers. Which brings us back to Snyder's reflection on 'all those years and their moments' shared with Lew Welch, captured in the kitchen where Snyder, his family and friends 'still laugh and cook'. The experience, whether expressed or unexpressed, becomes part of the cumulative total of those moments, the sum of human perceptions. Some of us are in need of time to digest this somewhat unexpected outcome from our discussions. Meantime, emerging from the snug, like Dante we turn again to see the stars.

Letter from Wales

SAM ADAMS

Joan, my late sister and elder by a dozen years, small, daintily proportioned and quite fearless, was a keen and accomplished horsewoman. Her favourite was a roan mare, a big hunter that would look down its long nose at her and do her bidding without demur. During the war years, when Joan worked in a vast and vitally important munitions factory, whatever daylight free time was at her disposal she spent riding the moorland tops of the mining valleys, usually alone, for the release it gave and to clear her lungs of chemicals. I mention this because, early on, during one of these rides, about five miles west over the mountain from our home in Gilfach Goch, she came upon Llangeinor, a village with some 280 inhabitants at that time, on the banks of Afon Garw, which drains one of the lesser fingers of the 'glove-shaped' Glamorgan valleys in Auden's poem. Friendships made and sustained there resulted in the Llangeinor hunt, a colourful moil of horses and hounds, assembling on post-war Boxing Days in the yard of the Griffin, the pub she and her husband kept by the hump-backed bridge over the branch line at Hendreforgan.

That recollection was triggered by an interesting coincidence. Recently I came across a newspaper advertisement for the sale of 'Tynton', a house and twenty-six-acre smallholding in Llangeinor. Photographs revealed a near derelict seventeenth-century property set among trees on the hillside above the village – just the sort of place where, in her riding days, my sister would have called to water the horse at a trough and probably have welcomed a drink to quench her own thirst. More properly *Ty'n y Ton* ('house in the fallow land'), it is Grade II listed but has been neglected for a considerable time and unoccupied in recent years. Within a day or so, our London daily carried particulars of a leasehold, seventeenth-century terraced property in Newington Green, N16, altogether grander in appearance it must be conceded, and at two and half million pounds, five times the asking price of the farmhouse and land in Glamorgan. But they are connected by a glistening thread.

'Tynton' was the family home of Richard Price, son of Rees Price, a dissenting minister, and his wife Catherine. He was born there a smidgen more than 300 years ago, 23 February 1723, and (Oxbridge denied him) educated in dissenting academies, including that of Vavasor Griffiths at Chancefield, near Talgarth, Breconshire. In 1740, aged seventeen, following the death of his parents, he proceeded to the Congregational Fund Academy, also known as Moorfields, in London, in all probability prompted and assisted by his father's younger brother, Samuel Price, already a resident there as co-pastor to that most prolific of hymn-writers Dr Isaac Watts. The young man remained a student at the academy until 1744 when, again almost certainly at the insistence of his uncle, he became chaplain to the Streatfield family of Stoke Newington. The connection is manifest in the Will of George Streatfield, Gent. (1682–1757) by which Samuel Price was bequeathed one hundred pounds. That Richard Price earned the esteem and affection of his patron is also clear from the same document, in which he was initially left two hundred pounds and, in a codicil of 1752, another three hundred pounds – 'over and besides what I have given to him in and by my said Will... provided he lives with me at the time of my decease'. When that occurred in June 1757, the bequest amounted to not far short of a quarter of a million in today's values. Soon afterwards Price married Sarah Blundell of Belgrave, Leicestershire and, as minister at the long-established meeting house, now Unitarian Church, on Newington Green (where Mary Wollstonecraft drew inspiration from his sermons), in 1758 he bought that fine house close by, 'part of the earliest brick-built terrace in London', now on the market once more. It was and is a quite splendid family home, but there were no children of the union.

Price was still in his early thirties and comfortably settled, but if the temptation to relax routinely into his pastoral role ever arose, he firmly repressed it. In the decades that followed, through his sermons, publications and the penetrating power of his intellect he made an immediate and lasting impact on the thinking and actions of others in two fields. Firstly, having edited and taken forward work on 'the Doctrine of Chances' by his friend the mathematician Thomas Bayes, in 1765 he was made a Fellow of the Royal Society, and in 1768 as an adviser to the Society for Equitable Assurances (now, familiarly, 'Equitable Life') he devised a system for 'Calculating the Values of Assurances on Lives'. Continuing in this vein, in 1771 he published 'Schemes for Providing Annuities for Widows'.

These essentially statistical propositions aimed at alleviating human problems still have currency, if in modified form, but their impact cannot compare with that of Price's contribution to political thought. His *Observations on the Nature of Civil Liberty, the Principles of Government, and the Justice and Policy of the War with America* was published at the beginning of 1776 and sold sixty thousand copies in the first year. It was widely translated and initiated contact with leading political figures in France, including the enlightened aristocrats Turgot and Nicolas de Condorcet, and in England, Thomas Paine, Joseph Priestley and the prison reformer John Howard. The transatlantic response was even warmer than he could have anticipated. The pamphlet arrived in America still in the early stages of the War of Independence and in good time for the Declaration of Independence on the fourth of July that same year. In the next decade Price gained the regard and friendship of some of the most venerated American thinkers and politicians, including Benjamin Franklin, who lived in London between 1757 and 1775 and was a frequent visitor at the house on Newington Green, Thomas Jefferson, and John Adams while he was American ambassador in London. Congress conferred on him honorary citizenship of the United States and asked him to assist in the development of its financial and economic policy, an invitation he declined with regret. In 1781, he and George Washington received the degree of Doctor of Laws from Yale. Curiously perhaps, he also received the Freedom of the City of London.

While Price remained in good health he would ride daily for the exercise and, afflicted perhaps by *hiraeth* (that peculiarly Welsh longing for home), he paid return visits to Llangeinor. Following the death of his wife in 1786, he moved to a new property in Hackney, where his widowed sister joined him. We are told his intellect remained as sharp as ever but eventually the ailments that accompanied ageing restricted his movements and 'depressed his spirits'. He died on 19 April 1791 and is buried at the Nonconformist burial ground Bunhill Fields, Islington. John Davies, the Welsh historian, sums him up simply: 'the most original thinker ever born in Wales'.

Snow Leopard and Dark-Iris Lakes

STAV POLEG

Because I'm not sure how long the main character
is planning to stay – in fact, he's just walked out
to watch the fireworks flowering turquoise and green
as the snow gets heavier and bright – let's just say that for a long-distance
runner and an occasional sprinter, he's one of those erratic treasures
with eyes so intensely cerulean and wild –
one could safely embark on a starship adventure to a far off
planet, knowing those deep, shiny irises will be visible
from space. Two astonishing lakes –
the kind that would turn you into a believer
in distance and play. Soon you will take a crash course
in wild swimming and deep-water
diving, soon you will learn to construct a spaceship
equipped with an advanced telescope lens to help you cope
with the mounting contradiction of velocity and longing
once leaving becomes the inevitable conclusion
of testing out space. You will learn how to bring distant objects
closer – rivers, cities, forests – closer
like the highway spiralling out of a faraway kingdom
you found yourself running around. Back
to our runner – he's based on an ex
of a neighbour who used to be a friend of a colleague
until something (everything) happened – we can study this
forever, but the fireworks are getting louder and the snow
has covered all the lakes, the forests and the villages –
throwing them into a further, harder-to-imagine distance
full of countries wrestling with latitude
and maps. How beautiful
the sky tonight – the way it's shimmering with dark –
and even though the snow is turning into a full-scale
blizzard, you might be able to detect
the woman practicing cartwheel after cartwheel
in the playing field outside. Some describe her
as the girl with the gift for gymnastics and singing
in crowds. Others struggle with her inconvenient tendency
to speak her mind. In any case, you'll recognise
her hard-to-pin-down accent. She's based on three
best friends, two rivers, a long-lost tormented lover, an autumnal
moon poised above a red-oak forest, a skylight
half open to the dark, a snow leopard, a midnight
thunderstorm, an unsent letter, a romantic train guard
holding a rose in a busy train station, a maple leaf on a silver
pavement, a grand piano on the seventh floor, and an entire
country whose borders have been fluctuating
for centuries, and she carries them all

with such burning intensity, there's a very real risk
she'll soon be burning the story she's about to lead, throwing
the ashes into a raging river from some glittering
Eastern European bridge just as the blue autumn
leaves start to blend with the first
signs of snow – a case of a character bigger
than all kinds of storms and sudden weather, stronger
than any towering bridge, wilder than the ever-changing
map of Eastern Europe before, between and after
the war/s, and while I know
you'd rather head back to those delicious
blue lakes – and I'm totally with you on that – I must
introduce you to another character, the one who's rarely
running late. You might want to reach
for a few bracing cocktails before we kick off. Are you ready
to defy distance, matter, logics, the spectacular
fields of applied mathematics and theoretical physics
and watch how a brief course of events
turns into a chaos indefensibly long? In short,
please welcome our comrade – a devoted, fervent
socialist. I suspect he'd appreciate it if you stood up
when he enters the room. What a way to land back
in the wonder that is – say – England in the years leading
to 2019. Where shall we begin? Outside, a lightning storm
is spiralling the streets into a sequence of luminous
and pitch-dark scenes. As for our comrade, right –
another drink? Yes, he's a narcissist – you've
got it – yes, he's a little bit of a misogynist. Sure,
he's upper-middle class – but only
in this story, which is surreal *and* fictional – Everybody
Calm Down – he's based on five high-school friends, several
pious atheists, I mean – saints, twenty-six
hangovers, seven didactic lectures, the longest
summer heatwave recorded to date, the magnetic theatricality
of protest politics, a Sunday in Trafalgar Square, a promising
vegan deli, two pleasant pubs somewhere faraway
in the English countryside, a rose
as a symbol of – wait for it – dissent, a significant
proportion of the UK poetry scene, and a few
of my worst nightmares during those years, in which
for the first time, for some reason, I found myself running
in the streets of 1930s Krakow as if there was something or someone
I had to see. The massive distraction that is politics
has led us astray, yet again, from those deep beautiful
lakes, although I'm not sure the distraction is politics, it is
something else – not history, not ideology, not even
the dark luminous horses of populism soaring above
every river and bridge, nor the cries of sainthood
in the age of faux victimhood – no, it is something
else, darker than these. Although in this version,
the comrade will turn into a painter – an artist who believes
in Art for its own sake. We'll come back to this
later. For now, the mountains are covered with snow, the rivers
are flowing with shimmering frost. Listen, you are on a mission
to embark on a starship towards the deepest blue
lakes. You're focused and impatient – fasten
your seatbelt and don't be distracted – only a few more
characters to go: meet Dora, an uptight cello player with a tendency
to declare open season on cats. There's Val – a young
professional with a considerable past, Remi – French, Laura,
an Italian living in exile (her words), and finally –
a messenger. Yep, a real one. I'm still looking into

the practicalities of a downright divine
intervention, but in the meantime – I'd be up for testing
the ground. Is anyone pregnant? Is anyone up for
rolling in a field naked? Until we sort out
these questions, let me take you on a winter break
far away in Zakopane – a resort town in southern
Poland – somewhere
between 1922 and 1927. Let me know if you can see
the girl playing in the snow – she's strong
and muscular – there – you can tell it's her
by her wide, palest-green eyes, there's something
rebellious in the way she lets go
of her mother's hand, lifting her younger
brother up in the air, chasing
her cousins like a furious leopard. I had no idea
she could cartwheel like this. I'm not sure I recognise
her confidence, her uncontrolled laughter, her incredible
smile. She's stronger than anyone
around her – yes, I recognise that. I don't think she notices
me, and if she does, she could never imagine
being a grandmother one day. It would make her cartwheel
out of this fragile picture, catch the first train
and throw up. I want to tell her don't let go
of your mother's hand. I want to tell her you don't understand
what's about to happen – you're not stronger
or bigger than this place and sudden weather, the country
you will run away from is so much larger
than you – it won't even notice
when you're gone, neither
will it care, it won't bother to write down
your parents' and grandparents' names, the entirety
of your cousins and friends, there will be no
hand left to hold onto, no addresses, it will be up to you
to memorise these traces of places and names, and yes –
good luck with that. I want to tell her, listen – don't take it the wrong
way, but could you please go? I'm trying
to write a story with actual fireworks – I have a brilliant
set of characters, it was supposed to be
funny. Have you heard the one
about the zealous socialist believing in Art for its own sake? Me
neither! I'm in the process of devising some kind of a divine
intervention – a Socialist, a Saint and a Populist go into
a Stoppard play – something along these lines or
temperament, there's supposed to be a full-blown tension
between Dora and Remi – the latter arrived two hours
ago, and already attracts a hell of a lot of attention,
there's a strong possibility that someone becomes miraculously
pregnant, even though I haven't worked out
why Laura is in exile, why Val is rereading the same
letter while chain-smoking all night, there are some unresolved
issues with flying cello strings and a few alarmed
cats, but instead of sorting them out I'm pushing
the door open and walking outside, raising the night
like a glass – holding this fear like a country
changing its mind or its borders, a snowstorm erasing
all traces and maps. I want to tell her, look –
there are two delicious cerulean lakes my readers
would really appreciate if I could finally
lead them to. It was a promise I made – not only to them
but to myself – that I shall not be distracted –
and I've just completed the most elegant starship
fitted with telescopes, cameras, long-distance

fire and snow, you see – there's this blue-eyed absolute
treasure – he was supposed to symbolise the aesthetically-pleasing
tension between a growing, unbearable distance
and the shattering impracticality of creative
attention – he's based on an ex of a neighbour who
used to be, well – the short story
is – would you mind taking back your, our
history and placing it on some random steep mountain or a faraway
bridge, maybe drop it into a raging Eastern European river by mistake,
would you stop repeating all those cousins' and friends' and
parents' names, I'm building a starship, I'm taking us
back to where it feels safest, I'm taking us back
to the lakes.

El Puerto de Guadarrama

JANE DURAN

'Tengo de pasar el puerto, el puerto de Guadarrama,
déjame pisar la nieve que pisó la serrana.'

'I have to walk through the pass, the Guadarrama pass.
Let me step on the snow where the mountain girl walked.'

On 28 March 2023 the moving folksong *El Puerto de Guadarrama* was performed by the guitarist Samuel Diz and sung by the tenor Jonatan Alvarado at the Residencia de Estudiantes in Madrid, at an event entitled *'Música y Poesía en la Residencia, del Mediterráneo de Cavafis al de Gustavo Durán'.* The event drew together three strands of my father's story: his music; his role as a Republican officer in the Spanish Civil War; and, towards the end of his life, his translations of Cavafy's poetry.

My father's source for the words and melody of *El Puerto de Guadarrama* was the *Cancionero musical popular español*, the songbook compiled by Felipe Pedrell, one of Spain's foremost collectors of folk music. The harmonies and arrangement for the song were composed by my father for the piano in Cuba in June 1944, just a few months before my birth in Havana. Its musical notation in his meticulous handwriting, together with his other musical compositions, letters and photographs, are all conserved in the Gustavo Durán Archive at the Residencia de Estudiantes in Madrid.

But the song, so full of longing, has other associations for me. Republican troops sang this at the front during the Spanish Civil War. The Guadarrama is a mountain range just north of Madrid, forming a natural defence for the city and seat of government; when sections of Spain's army rose up against the Republic, the Sierra of Guadarrama became an early site of fierce resistance and battle. The song also brings to my mind that well-known photograph of Republican militiamen surrendering to rebel troops in the Somosierra Pass on the Guadarrama front in August 1936.

The longing that comes through the melody and words of *El Puerto de Guadarrama* also, for me, evokes a landscape in a homeland denied to my father after the Republican army was defeated in 1939. My father, Gustavo Durán, died on 26 March 1969 at the age of sixty-two, almost to the day thirty years after he went into exile at the end of the Spanish Civil War. In all that time he had never been able to return to Spain. He wanted us, his three daughters, to know Spain and his family, but we had to visit his country without him. Although he had found refuge in the United States, new struggles awaited him there: he suffered continuous investigations by the FBI and persecution by Senator McCarthy, stemming from his role and affiliations as a Republican officer in the war.

Most evenings when my father returned home after work, he would sit down at the piano and play, or compose his arrangements of folk songs, many of them Spanish. This was what he loved doing and where he was truly in his element. In the New York of my childhood and adolescence, the families of Spanish exiles gathered, often at the apartment of the García Lorcas on Riverside Drive. A moment invariably arrived when everyone would sing Spanish folk songs, simple, strange and beautiful in their melodies and imagery. Born in Barcelona in 1906, Gustavo had trained as a pianist in Madrid and Paris. By the age of seventeen, when he was a regular visitor to the Residencia de Estudiantes, he was already composing music in a classical idiom.[1]

Alberto Jiménez Fraud founded the Residencia de

1 Some of these pieces can be heard on the album *Canción de arte* (1999, ARCIS)

Estudiantes in Madrid in 1910. His vision for this was influenced by the educational ethos of the reformist *Institución Libre de Enseñanza* (Institute of Independent Education) founded by Francisco Giner de los Ríos in 1876. The Residencia encouraged openness to liberal European culture and became a hub for international academic exchange. It offered university students from different parts of Spain not only accommodation, but a cultural centre, a place of learning and interdisciplinary dialogue.

Its second and permanent site was on the *Cerro del Viento* (Hill of the Wind) – later renamed the *Colina de los Chopos* (Hill of Poplars) by the poet Juan Ramón Jiménez – on the northern outskirts of Madrid. The new 'pavilions' of the Residencia were constructed in a neo-Mudéjar style, and Juan Ramón Jiménez designed and directed the planting of its poplars and garden of oleanders. Students were housed in austerely-furnished rooms: the poet Rafael Alberti described Lorca's room as 'Almost a cell, cheerful, bright... And everything close to hand: flower, tree, sky, water... the Guadarrama already with no snow.'[2]

A vibrant intellectual and artistic life developed among its students and visitors. Among its illustrious residents were Federico García Lorca (who arrived there in 1919), Salvador Dalí, Luis Buñuel, the poet Emilio Prados, composers Ernesto and Rodolfo Halffter and the scientist Severo Ochoa; while visitors Miguel de Unamuno, Manuel de Falla, the philosopher José Ortega y Gasset, poets Pedro Salinas and Rafael Alberti, and physicist Blas Cabrera y Felipe were drawn into its orbit.

One of the salons had a grand piano, and students and visitors gathered there for musical evenings. In the early decades of the twentieth century there was a resurgence of interest in the folksongs and ballads of Spain: musicologists such as Ramón Menéndez Pidal, Eduardo Martínez Torner and the composer Manuel de Falla who collaborated with Lorca in this mission, devoted themselves to researching and rescuing traditional Spanish song. In his book *Prosas* (1980), the poet Rafael Alberti wrote: 'That Pleyel [piano] in the Residencia! Afternoons and evenings spent around its keyboard in the spring and the beginnings of summer, hearing all the hidden riches rise from its profound river, all the diverse voice of Spain, deep, sad, agile and joyous... Before that piano I have witnessed delightful folkloric challenges – or rather examinations – between Lorca, Ernesto Halffter, Gustavo Durán, all very young then, and some residents already familiar with our songbooks.'[3]

In the poetry of Lorca there are echoes, or even lines quoted from these traditional songs and ballads. Although no recordings of the voice of Lorca have come to light yet, there is a recording made in 1931 of the famous singer 'La Argentinita', Encarnación López, singing traditional Spanish songs, accompanied by Lorca at the piano playing his own arrangements. One of the strong affinities between Lorca and my father was their shared interest in and love of Spanish folk music.

A close friendship developed between Lorca, my father, Alberti and the filmmaker Luis Buñuel. The interaction between artists, musicians and poets connected with the Residencia inspired creativity and often exciting collaborations. My father's first known musical composition, *El corazón de Háfiz*, was dedicated to Lorca, and Lorca's poem *Friso* (Frieze) to my father in his book *Canciones* (Songs). Alberti asked three young composers, Rodolfo Halffter, Ernesto Halffter and my father,to each write a song inspired by a poem in his collection *Marinero en tierra*. The three musical scores appeared in the published book in 1925, as well as a cover drawing by the painter Daniel Vásquez Díaz. The book included a poem, *Pirata*, dedicated to my father. In 1932 my father accompanied Buñuel and Alberti to Las Hurdes in Cáceres, Extremadura, on a research trip in preparation for Buñuel's film 'Land Without Bread' (*Tierra Sin Pan*) – his searing exposure of rural poverty.

When Franco's colonial troops were airlifted from Morocco to the Spanish peninsula in planes supplied by Nazi Germany and Fascist Italy in July 1936, my father's life changed utterly. He joined the railway militia in defence of the besieged Republic, serving on an armoured train in the Sierra of Guadarrama. His friend Pablo de la Fuente described the train in his book *Sobre Tierra Prestada* (On Borrowed Soil): 'It was the first solid armament of our front to the north of Madrid. When the train appeared firing its little canons and hiding in the tunnels to protect itself from the aviation, it raised the morale of the militia, and broke the surprised morale of the rebels. They had been told that we were unarmed and no threat, and they were confronted with that enormous machine, with that deafening and formidable dragon.'[4] Pablo's inscription to my father in a copy of *Sobre Tierra Prestada* evokes their participation in the defence of Madrid.

At the orders of the Republican high command Gustavo went on to lead a number of important military units, fighting in the strategic battles of Jarama, La Granja (Segovia) and Brunete. He also worked closely with the *Alianza de Intelectuales Antifascistas* to gain support for the Republican cause through the arts. In July 1937 he received orders to form the 47th Division. This Division fought in Teruel (Aragón) in north-east Spain during the bitter winter of 1937–8, a turning point in the war. After the Republican defeat at Teruel, Franco's army launched an offensive through Aragón and Castellón, and the exhausted, depleted Republican troops retreated over the arid and rocky terrain of the Maestrazgo mountain range while continuing to resist the oncoming forces. In May 1938 my father was promoted to Lieutenant Colonel and commanded the 20th Army Corps of the Levante in a defence that prevented Franco's troops from conquering Valencia.

At the end of the war he was one of the luckier ones who escaped. He left Spain aboard a British naval vessel from the port of Gandía in Valencia and found refuge in England. There he met my mother – Bonté Crompton, an American – at Dartington Hall and they married and moved to the United States. In an interview published in the Argentinian magazine *Tribuna* in 1945, my father said: 'In London I began to rebuild my life. A brief physical rest.

2 R. Alberti, *Prosas*, Alianza Editorial, Madrid, 1980, p.157. All translations in this essay are by the author.

3 R. Alberti, *Prosas*, p.91

4 P. de la Fuente, *Sobre Tierra Prestada*, Ediciones 'Nuestro Tiempo', Santiago, Chile, 1946, p.115

I made a resolution not to speak about the Civil War until new days arrived'.[5] He didn't speak to us, his daughters, about his experience of that war. It was a topic that nobody mentioned, nor did we ask him about it.

Years after our father died I read an essay about Teruel that he wrote for Robert Payne's collection of eyewitness accounts, *The Civil War in Spain*. The piece was anonymous, he was simply described as 'an officer of the Republican Army'. Why did he want to remain anonymous? 'Our object was to take La Muela de Teruel, the flat-topped hill on the south bank of the Guadalaviar River, overlooking Teruel... The horror was in the cold, the wind, the snow, the absence of footholds. More than half our casualties came from frostbite: many had to have their toes amputated... Teruel is the coldest town in Spain, but the hill was colder. La Muela was absolutely barren: no trees, no grasses, grew on it. All around Teruel there is this eroded land with deep gulleys, harsh and uninviting. But we clung to our hill.'[6]

I began to think about my father's silence about the war, and wanted to explore this through poetry. I began to research the war itself, at first so remote: 'I can scarcely imagine it happened – / where it would be – the places of it. / Quiet places I visit now – torn up grass, / headed-off mist, depositions / of rose, vine, earth...'[7] But it came into clearer focus slowly. I visited the Muela of Teruel where there were still remnants of battle trenches and broken ceramics, and saw how bleak and unforgiving it was; and the ruins of Belchite, bombed so heavily the town had to be entirely rebuilt on a separate site. I walked in the Maestrazgo mountains and spoke with older villagers about the war, still present in their lives. I began to piece out a map of a book that became *Silences from the Spanish Civil War* (Enitharmon, 2002). I wanted the poems to be spare and for silence to pervade them.

Maestrazgo

The deeper I go in the wind
the more unreal the days of departure
till I reach a look-out point
over distant farmhouses, sheepfolds

and see the waterline of the mountain range
as if it were part of me,
the friendliness and force it exerts on me.

My father said goodbye. He joined the militia.
Everything is lifted up and dries.
It is a long way down
from all parched things.

A bilingual edition of my book was published in Spain by Renacimiento in 2019.[8] Gloria García Lorca (niece of the poet) and I read from her translations of my poems at the 2023 Residencia event commemorating my father. Gloria's translations are so faithful and sensitive that it's as if the poems were originally written in Spanish. Our close friendship dates from childhood, and together we collaborated on translating Lorca's *Gypsy Ballads*, his *Tamarit Diván* and *Sonnets of Dark Love*, published here as bilingual editions by Enitharmon Press..

The third strand of my father's story which formed part of the 2023 Residencia event concerned his translations of poems by the Greek poet Cavafy. In 1946 Gustavo joined the United Nations, the beginning of a long career, with postings to Chile and the Congo. His final posting was in Greece, a return to the Mediterranean. There he learned to speak Greek fluently and began to read Greek poetry. In a letter written in Spanish to my sister Cheli in 1967, he spoke of his wish to translate 'into my own language, that which others had the luck of creating'. He explained that he had read Palamas, Sikelianos, Elytis, Seferis and Cavafy, but that he had chosen the poetry of Cavafy: 'in the first place because, although like all great poets he lives in a hermetic world, his expression is not cryptic, or at least, not as cryptic as that of Seferis; and secondly, because his lyricism, if not deeper, is more original, mysterious and reticent than that of the other poets I have named. Finally, because I like the inflection of irony in his style. Even when it is at its most sombre, a subtly sceptic smile appears or is glimpsed in his verses.'[9]

Gustavo sent his Spanish translations to his friend, the poet Jaime Gil de Biedma, in Barcelona. Some years after my father's death, Jaime gave the folder of poems to the poet Alejandro Duque Amusco. In 2018 Alejandro began the work of gathering and editing these in a book called *Días finales en Grecia* (Final days in Greece) which was published by Pre-Textos in 2019. Alejandro read some of these fine, musical translations at the Residencia event. The folder also contained the only poem written by my father that has come to light, called *Con el dedo en los labios* (With my finger to my lips), another silence. The folder is now in my father's archive at the Residencia.

My father died in Athens in 1969, only days before he was due to retire from the United Nations. He had been planning to return to Spain for the first time. He is buried in Alones, a small village in the mountains of Crete. My mother told me that on the night before he died he had been reading *Don Quijote* and laughing.

My sister Lucy Durán, a Professor of Music at SOAS in London, continues to research our father's compositions, working in collaboration with the Spanish guitarist Samuel Diz and the Argentinian tenor Jonatan Alvarado, who have to date recorded four of his songs on their album *Memoria de la Melancolía*, including *El Puerto de Guadarrama.*[10] Together they are slowly docu-

5 *Tribuna* , Rosario, 18/9/45; cited in J. Juárez, *Comandante Durán*, Debate, Barcelona, 2009, p.266

6 R. Payne, *The Civil War in Spain*, Secker and Warburg, London, 1963, p.291–2

7 J. Duran, *Silences from the Spanish Civil War*, Enitharmon, 2002, p.26

8 J. Durán, *Silencios desde la guerra civil española*, Editorial Renacimiento, Sevilla, 2019

9 Letter to Cheli Durán cited in *Días finales en Grecia*, Edición de A. Duque Amusco, Pre-Textos, Madrid, 2019

10 *Memoria de la Melancolía* (2020, Poliédrica)

menting and recording his post-war music in a project they call *Cancionero de Gustavo Durán* (The Gustavo Durán Songbook). These are short compositions based on folksong, mainly from the Spanish-speaking world, with his original piano accompaniments, inspired by many *cancioneros*. Lucy believes that when 'Gustavo played these beautiful ballads on the piano, while family and friends stood around him and sang, in fact this was our father's coded way of breaking his silence without inviting comment. Those bittersweet folk ballads were his hidden form of sharing memories of his colourful life from before the Spanish Civil War, his loves and losses, regrets and joys. This was not achieved just through the lyrics of the folk ballads – often very poignant – but also through his minimalist piano arrangements tinged with subtle dissonance, reflecting influences from his favourite composers, especially Falla, Ravel and Mompou.'

Our father's friend from Residencia days, the poet Emilio Prados, in exile in Mexico, wrote to him in 1956: 'I am old now but the same inside, absolutely the same as I was when we walked around the old Madrid... My life is entirely dedicated to poetry, and so, like you I am happy to live it with its shadows and its light. I am alive, now yes, as Federico used to say to you, do you remember?: in almost a cell, in the city, not on the hill; but from there, as I told you in our first conversations, I vibrate in my own way, with my form of love or madness, in the beautiful universe. What more do I want?'[11]

Among my books is *Sobre Tierra Prestada* (On Borrowed Soil) by Pablo de la Fuente, the friend who served with my father on that armoured train in the Guadarrama in the early days of the war, and whose brother died in the battle of the Ebro. Pablo's book, now falling apart in my hands, was published in 1946 in Chile where Pablo was living in exile. On the title page his scribbled dedication reads: 'For Gustavo Durán, these impressions of our finest days...' The book narrates Pablo's experience of a Madrid under siege and his own journey into exile, and ends with these words: 'We cannot be reborn now. The trunk of our life is there: our brothers defend it with their blood, so that we may once again feel the sap that we will never find while we are in transit and on borrowed soil.'[12]

11 Letter from E. Prados to G. Durán, 29 October, 1956, Archivo Gustavo Durán, Residencia de Estudiantes

12 P. de la Fuente, *Sobre Tierra Prestada*, Ediciones 'Nuestro Tiempo', Santiago, Chile, 1946, p.298

Under a Strange Shadow

An interview with poet and translator Oksana Maksymchuk

SASHA DUGDALE

Sasha Dugdale: Can you tell me about your childhood in Soviet Ukraine? I'm keen to hear how it felt to you growing up in the stagnating air of the late USSR, especially as the child of a dissident actor working and living in Lviv, the centre of a Ukrainian cultural revival during this period. Was there a large gap between private and public realities?

Oksana Maksymchuk: It's fascinating how the stagnation of one culture creates the conditions for the revival or reinvention of another, isn't it? As a child, I had a sharp sense that the inner family world was very different from the official outer world, and that the traffic between them needed to be tightly controlled. Growing up in the Soviet Union involved leading a double life, defined, from a child's perspective, by a nightmarish economy of punitive mechanisms: my parents warned me that if we weren't vigilant about what we said outside of our home, they could be arrested, and I would be put in an orphanage. At the same time I think they knew that you could only expect so much from a kid, and they tended to self-censor so that I wouldn't unintentionally reveal their secrets. There were plenty of stories of such incidents – sometimes because a child had made a mistake or had been bribed, at other times because a child genuinely thought they were doing the right thing in reporting on their parents. We, the children, were often given examples from literature and Soviet hagiography, and the child who chose the State over the Family was always portrayed as a hero ('Nothing great is ever easy!'). So it would have been foolish for a parent not to prepare for any eventuality.

The first experience of the dissociation between the inner and the outer world that I remember very distinctively was this: I was three or four, and for a celebration of the Great October, or maybe International Workers' Day, I was assigned to read a short poem, in Russian:

I am a little girl
I don't go to school yet
I have never seen Lenin
but I love him very much.

The poem was simple, it rhymed, and it was in a language I perceived as both serious and foreign, the language that unified 'all twelve sister-republics' (a line from another poem I cherished); I delighted in my future performance and kept practising reciting the poem around our tiny apartment. My father didn't say anything then, but a couple of weeks later, as I was greeting guests at the door and making small talk (how I'd grown, what I was learning at day-care) he spontaneously recited the poem I'd been practising, imitating my childish pathos. And everyone laughed! It felt like they were laughing at me, and at Lenin. I remember, mostly, getting flustered and really, deeply hating my father. Years later, in first grade (1989), as we read story after story about Lenin's heroic feats in our Russian-language textbooks, the teacher said that no man in the world deserved our affection and admiration as much as he did (he was still on display at the Mausoleum in Moscow, and every young pioneer's dream was to visit his relics and pay tribute). I raised my hand and announced in front of the whole class that I didn't love Lenin. I was taking back those earlier poetic words of devotion – initiating an anti-baptism, rescinding a promise to love and obey. The original recitation of the poem was like a spell, and I had decided to break it, exorcising myself. By that time, I had already been promoted to a young Octobrist, in two more years I'd become a Pioneer. After the lesson, I was taken to the headteacher's office and reprimanded. A year or two later, in 1990 or 1991, a few of the girls from my class approached me at break time and said: 'Remember that time you said you didn't love Lenin? We don't love him either.'

Had the Putsch in 1991 been successful, had the USSR prevailed, what then? I think I would have gone back to keeping my mouth shut, going through the motions. Performative conformism was a condition for pursuing one's studies, for getting a job. So I would have enacted the role – as most of my family members had done, with varying success.

Tell me about your proximity to the theatre and the effect it had on you as a girl. Your father was a well-known actor at a time when theatre was a leading force in cultural dissent in the USSR. Soviet theatres also had a very collective feel as they were repertory, the actors often lived and worked together for years and they forged creative and personal bonds which are hard to imagine in the West. Were you the child of an extended 'theatre family'? And how has the art-form affected your own creativity?

You're so right that a theatre collective resembles a family: people love and support each other as much as they fight and compete, gossip and scheme. I remember when it seemed to be the funnest, freest place in the world – actors came across as much more emotionally complex and authentic than the average Soviet citizen.

Growing up in the theatre further normalised dissociation, a splintering of identity, impressing upon me that in different spheres in life, we may be called upon to play different roles. I learned that when a person I know is acting out of character, for instance, it's because they're currently enacting another script, navigating a virtual situation which may be incomprehensible to others. In this domain, my earliest memory also dates back to early childhood. This must have been one of the first times I went to see my father 'at work', and I was terrified: Tato was in trouble, he was being confronted on the stage! Suddenly a shot rang out. I was beside myself and began screaming – Tato fell on his knees, then collapsed. My immediate thought was that he was being punished because I'd said something 'prohibited'. It was just as I'd been warned: Tato was dead, and now I'd be put in a children's home!

When I was cast in the role of Macduff's young son, my father began coaching me. I often recited verses from memory, and he'd help me adjust my diction, timing, rhythm, intonation and so on. We only worked on one piece at a time, which I would then go on to perform at school functions and recitation competitions. In fact this early practice became a hindrance and it took me years to shed my dramatic training; to unlearn the exaggerated articulateness, and chiselled diction. My preferred mode of 'enacting a poet' emphasises vulnerability and discomfort. I don't wish to smooth over the difficult parts: I want to expose the resistance and strangeness of the material.

Father didn't just work at the theatre. Our first home as a family was a tiny studio in the theatre courtyard. My mother, a medical doctor, thought it was very romantic. When I was two, we were finally assigned an apartment in a brand new fourteen-storey building. There were three fourteen-story buildings in a single row, like a triple rhyme. We got a corner apartment on the thirteenth floor, overlooking an expanse of private houses with gardens known as the Warsowian district, with a church in the middle and low rolling hills in the distance. And the vast, vast sky!

My father had started expanding his circle of friends beyond the theatre when he was still a student in Kharkiv. He sought out writers, artists and intellectuals and over his lifetime he befriended many of the most prominent figures in Ukrainian culture. Some of his friends had been imprisoned and got out, and some were still in the camps when I was growing up. There was a distinctive sense that the people we knew were not what they appeared – that despite their blemished biographies and menial day jobs, these were giants who'd change our world, and there was an aura of transgression and excitement about their work.

Our apartment was tiny and yet it was regularly packed with up to half a hundred people for various occasions – birthdays, holidays, spontaneous celebrations when someone got out of prison or was allowed to publish after years of state-sanctioned ostracism. I remember a lot of laughter, giddiness, joy and levity – even though so many of our guests had a virtual sword of Damocles hanging over their heads. Poems were read, toasts were offered, the guests were dressed up, sometimes even in costumes.

As a prominent dissident was your own father touched by the waves of repression?

Father had a series of direct confrontations with the authorities, and he had been tailed by the KGB since the late sixties. One of his close friends had turned out to have been an informer, appointed specifically to keep an eye on him. His performances were regularly cancelled and he was denied promotions and roles. But unlike many of his friends, my father was never arrested, and this was a source of unease for him. When so many people in his circle had been arrested and he hadn't, this naturally led to suspicion: was he cooperating with the secret services or were they just trying to sow distrust? My great-aunt, who had been married to a KGB general, told me her version a decade ago in Kherson, where she still lives: her husband, my mother's uncle, upon learning that my father was about to be indicted, travelled incognito to Lviv, and 'edited' his file. When I told my father, he winced. If not getting arrested tormented him, the narrative of getting saved by a KGB general certainly didn't ease his discomfort.

Your own poetry must have been affected by this miraculous childhood, surrounded by elite cultural figures who must have treated you as one of their kind. What were your first attempts to write?

Looking back on my earliest childhood attempts at composing poetry, I realise that they usually emerged as an attempt to improve something I found slightly 'off' or lacking. I often changed poems as I performed them, substituting words and rhymes, sometimes reinventing whole stanzas, altering their order. I also owned a large collection of illustrated children's books – my parents insisted these were my most treasured possessions (I did not agree!) – and occasionally I'd have a feeling that a poem didn't live up to the illustration, so I'd rewrite the poem. My first recognition as a poet dates back to an afterschool programme in primary school. I wrote a tightly-rhymed poem about a picture I saw in a book: a large bunny on a tractor, looking out of the window (breaking the fourth wall!). My friend Olia was waiting for me to finish, her elbows on my desk. We were both giggling as I read the verses to her, and so the teacher came over, and when she saw what I'd done, she took the notebook and darted off. My friend and I thought we must be in trouble and we hid under the desk. The teacher returned with a colleague, and they sat down with us and edited the poem, but only slightly: how about instead of this line, where you say that a bunny is gulping water out of the well like a junkie (*narcoman*), we say that the bunny is *drawing* water out of the well for his thirsty family? Wouldn't this be a better way of describing an industrious bunny on a collective farm? I should add that *narcomania* was a new widely-discussed social issue at the time. Playing Hopscotch and Elastics, we would exchange scary stories about junkies catching you to plunge a needle into you, either to draw your blood or to inject a dangerous substance into your bloodstream. Just that summer, Grandma Olena, my father's mother, had found her poppy patch vandalised, the unripe poppy heads missing, white juice seeping from the stems. I drew on that context to compose the poem, and unexpectedly experienced my first act of censorship.

You write poetry in both English and Ukrainian, but your most recent work is in English. How did that come about and what was the transition point – the moment that gave you the sense that you needed to respond to your surroundings in a new language?

When I moved to the States in 1997, I signed up for a poetry class – sensing, correctly, that it would help me with my transition to the new language. I went on to publish in our high school's journal *Unique* every year – I wrote my poems right before the submission deadline, dropped them into the envelope taped to a classroom door, and most of them ended up in print. My high school was highly selective and very competitive, and I was at a disadvantage, a non-resident alien with no money for college, so I was trying to build up my CV.

In college, I went back to writing poems in Ukrainian. My first serious publication, with an introduction by Andriy Sodomora, the foremost living translator of Latin poetry and philosophy into Ukrainian and a prominent poet and essayist in his own right, appeared when I was nineteen; it was a portfolio of ten poems, and it made me feel like a rock-star. I remember going to parties and getting introduced as 'a published Ukrainian poet' – a mysterious, lofty outsider. This feeling of distinction counterbalanced some of the struggles I was facing: I was poor, working three campus jobs (as a waitress, a grader for calculus, and a Language Learning Laboratory administrator); and because my mother was still fighting to secure papers for us, I couldn't travel back home for six long years.

Could you say a little about the language politics during the period of your childhood in Lviv? As you've said, Lviv was a thriving centre for Ukrainian culture and language within an enormous Soviet empire with only one state language: Russian. What did this mean for everyday living in practice?

When I was growing up, everyone in my family only spoke Ukrainian, but such different dialects that to me they sounded like different languages. In Lviv, where I was born, my parents and I were outsiders – everyone was; it was practically a new city, demographically speaking, after the war. The Jewish third of the population had been exterminated under the German occupation or transferred to the camps, and the Polish half had been deported on Soviet orders. Of the original pre-war population, fewer than one-fifth remained in the city. But the surrounding villages were Ukrainian-speaking, so by the time I was born, Lviv was three-fourths Ukrainian. Nevertheless, Russian was the dominant language on TV; many of my books were in Russian. We children often tried speaking Russian to each other during playtime – all our curses and threats and spells and counting-out rhymes were in Russian, for instance. Later on, in the early nineties, when we started playing with Barbie dolls and watching foreign soap operas, almost universally dubbed in Russian, we would apply the melodramatic dialogues from the soaps to our games. It was a language of intrigue, and sex, and everything prohibited we weren't supposed to speak about – a language that held our dirty thoughts and adolescent anxieties.

By the time I was a teenager, I could read and write Russian with fluency, and went on to win awards in essay competitions in the native speaker category in the US. I've come to recognize this as a typical feature of the colonial predicament: the colonial subject learns to imitate the coloniser, to 'pass' in order to reap the privileges that accrue to the coloniser's power; but while her cultivation of fluency requires her to develop an intimate understanding of the coloniser, she herself remains outside the scope of the colonizer's gaze. She sees and she knows, yet she is unseen and unknown. This is one reason why some Ukrainians are reluctant to speak Russian, even if they know it: they refuse to pass, choosing to assert their difference.

When you began experimenting in English creative writing as a way to improve your English, did you find yourself trying to bend English to forms and themes you already held dear (as someone close to Ukrainian culture) or did the English take you in different ways, form new senses of self? I wonder if you encountered more freedom in your adopted language?

My first teenage attempts at writing in English felt like self-translation – poems borne out of a different register, from another world. Upon arriving in the US, I was overwhelmed with noise: the gurgling and hissing and roaring that was, I knew, a form of communication, and to which I was expected to respond. I was drawn to poetry, yes, but I didn't feel eloquent or deft. I did cheat a little, sneaking in a locution here and there from some Ukrainian poet I loved, which, I felt, elevated my writing, made it more distinguished and authoritative. Occasionally, I still splice a word or phrase into my poems, sometimes citing a poet by name, sometimes positioning my interlocutor generically, as 'a poet'. Even without such splicing, traces of foreign literary DNA inevitably make it into one's work: we learn by imitation, and we create through dialogical friction, exchange; it's an almost-erotic process: the Platonic reproduction in the presence of Beauty.

I do feel freer in my adopted language, as I do in my American identity – it's a more playful terrain for me. In Ukrainian, my poetry tends to be formally constrained: syllabo-tonic, tightly rhymed. Much of my energy is expended on coming up with innovative rhyming patterns, new types of line. The 'I' is more or less anonymized; it's hardly even gendered. In the tradition I chose to follow, you distinguish yourself and assert your uniqueness through a sort of technical mastery, which is fruitful and rewarding in its own way. By contrast, my English-language poetry is a form of storytelling, and its formal elements are subordinated to that purpose: to carry a story, to cast a spell. I give myself permission to be awkward and vulnerable, to get confused. In English, I'm also more likely to be charmed by the apparent flaws and imperfections in the work of others. When I switch to Ukrainian, I become an excruciatingly harsh critic – my optics and sensibilities really shift! Sometimes, I need to rewrite the poem in English in my mind to begin appreciating it.

And did the process of linguistic 'reckoning' change the relationship with Ukrainian?

Living in what felt like exile made Ukrainian a language of home and longing for me, a lost continent of coming-of-age. As an immigrant, I experienced a second childhood – I learned to talk and walk, to dress; to calibrate my sense of humour; to negotiate my rights, insist on my autonomy. The transition gave me a sense of an open future – and it also created a gap, like there was a parallel reality that I was no longer living. It was out of that painful, frustrating rupture that my poems emerged, as a way of asserting my presence in the world I'd lost, and that closed in around my absence without leaving a mark. I wanted to make sure there were traces, tracks, that would hold a place for me and allow me to make my way back, eventually.

You are now a translator and editor of Ukrainian poetry and so you are in a position of being a bridge between two cultures. You told me once that seeing a lot of contemporary poetry (particularly relating to war) has made you think about how you want to write about war. Could you say more about that?

One interesting aspect of writing and translating war poetry is that you're never alone: your voice is always already a part of a chorus. There are certain experiences that strip us of our defences, change our sense of temporality and spatiality, compel us to question what is real; what matters to us; and why. Love is often like that, but it overtakes us privately. By contrast, the experience of war is synchronic; and even though it can be terrifyingly private and isolating, it is also collective, unifying. You wouldn't wish the experience on anyone, but I also understand people who speak of war envy. What is bad for individuals may be good for communities, and what is bad for life may be good for art, and vice versa.

I started writing my own 'war poems' a year or two before the invasion, in 2011–12. But then the actual war started, and I lost my voice. When I did pick up again, it was in English, and I was living in Ukraine. As warnings of the full-scale invasion started coming in from abroad, I wrote poems out of that anxious waiting, feeling out the contours of what was already taking shape, but was still mostly invisible, inconceivable. I had, by that time, co-edited an anthology of contemporary war poetry (*Words for War*, published in 2017), and for that we'd sifted through thousands of texts, out of which we selected just over a hundred. So I was attuned to what other poets in Ukraine have been doing, often spontaneously, without knowing much about world war poetry or about witness poetry; without any conceptual frameworks or significant examples to guide them. Often, war-time writing is highly expressive, emotional, bound to the terrible moment it bears witness to. Writing in English creates, for me, the illusion of temporal distance, which allows me to speak in a freer, more even voice. I'm still learning how to speak about difficult, liminal experiences – experiences that force us into the realness we're all too ready to forgo for comfort or illusion of order – without distorting or flattening them into a clever artifice or a prolonged primordial scream.

Poems

OKSANA MAKSYMCHUK

My doll is more than
a faceless log

I dress it up in a rag
made out of a torn-up flag

I rock it back and forth
cradling it in my arms

I throw it up and kick it
like a soccer ball

Don't you love your doll?
the others ask

Yes yes
This is how we play

Wards of the state, we're cared for
by all
and no one

Human-faced
like a Sirin bird
the state throws food down its children's throats

We're kept warm
by the shreds of flesh buried beneath
our strong clawed feet

To each according to her
need, from each according to her
talon, declares the slogan

Recently but an egg
I bask in the heat, my feet
dance to a song

I'm a girl whose hand
nobody holds

In a choral circle
I dance alone

I enjoy the benefit
of the Law

submitting my body
to a purpose

Like a holy cloth
with markings of blood

I bear the stains of sainthood
on the outer circle of Love

On weekends we put on aprons
and kersey boots

Holding hands
we march out in rows

We whitewash trees in the spring
rake leaves in the fall

This is how we pay back our country
for what we owe

Overseers examine our work
give us cigarettes as a reward

Digging drainage, collecting garbage
we joke and smoke

Our leaders call it –a *subbotnik*

One among many
one with all

I dissolve in the form
of the communal body

A creature of many arms
many mouths

I occupy every room
in this hearthless house

A home of no walls
a borderless meadow

Spirit thirsting after
a greater freedom

A foreigner inside me
my tongue

forming words
I do not discern

sonic texture morphing
into crystals

shadows against the palate
roof opening to the sky

I spy
a beyond

silver linings of senses, slivers
of syllables

loose oscillating syntax
wet oily stars

ordered in constellations

On the outside
it sounds like

hissing

Marked in red –
our victories, unmarked –
the defeats

In the empty fields
our heroes remain
like sheaves of wheat

Willingly, we exchange
freedom for peace
arms for bread

All in white
hair in a braid
coiling around her head

Motherland emanates light

Marking out the rhythm
for a song, my throat
clutched by a steely grip
hoarse with the salty soil

whispers *Slava Slava*

Like a hollow doll
turned inside out
through a punctured hole

I dance in a dress of flesh
inner organs exposed
tied to me with a pulsing sash

Shrieking out
I dance
in a pool of blood

Inside me
my outer shell
crumpled up

a wrinkled balloon
waiting for a lung
to blow breath into it

Five Poems

SILIS MACLEOD

Leod's Dream

There was little feeling for an expedition.
The idea of the island was enough.
Breaking apart the hulls of their ships,

they warmed themselves by fireside,
eating what was left of the food
carried far from home. Then in a fit of foam

the island descended. Dragging
the garden to the dark of the sea.
Ideas do not float, they sink like pearls.

Cadahus, En son us. Sea birds bathe,
smoothing their feathers. You must
remember how awful it will be,

when the whole caste is fallen:
fish blood and fowl blood; the bird
bolted across the deep sea.

Children gathering pebbles on the shore
found a figure half-buried in the mud,
took her up, washed her, clothed her.

They taught the girl to spin
and to make
the sign of the cross.

All my fruit has dried and the fly hums
along the windowsill, unspooling the day.
Nothing isn't easy. No one

has pulled aside my curtains.
This grotto, fatal to most,
awful to all, accommodates little

coming or going. Did I dream
I was the fish?
Or did the fish dream itself me?

MacLean lies plume-plucked,
his sea calves sulking on the sand,
reduced to a sad and final shape.

This boat, the quickest ever from oak to oar,
or so he claims, rests upturned on the shore:
Leod's late brown rump.

Badbea 1792

Chunnacas na mairbh beó

we are not birds
blessed with wings
skilled at living
on high things

we are not fish
carving the foam
we are people
far from home

stone by stone
we have come
doing again
what was undone

gathering heather
to make a broom
cutting peat
to heat the room

we are not sheep
rich in wool
nor are we deer
high on the hill

we are like you
lairds of our place
a pile of stone
in an emptied space

Grass

greylags
descend
on the merse

to prattle
in the shelter
of an alder

tourists
echoes the
cattle farmer's

warning shot:
the grass
is the life

Gipsy Point

(latitude 54.76941, longitude -4.04571)

the colour
of the sea
is modified
by the particles
which float in it
by the angle

from which
it is viewed
by the clarity
of the day
by reflection
from the sky

the clouds
or adjacent cliffs
and in the shallows
by the colour
of the sea-floor
water has a
slightly bluish tint
a white object
sinking into
the water
turns blue
before passing

out of sight
finely divided
drops of water
always look
intensely white
so that the spray

from a breaking wave
is literally whiter
than snow

The Water Horse

from the Gaelic

Sometimes, into our lives,
comes the water horse –

an implausible stud,
with sand in his hair

and nothing but the deep
loch in his dark stare.

At the water's edge, he waits,
beckoning me forth.

Five Poems

IWAN LLWYD

Translated by Robert Minhinnick

Hen Gitar

All things must pass

I'm missing the Friday feelgood,
with that castle at Cricieth through the mist
like some poxy Welsh hat, and only
death's breaking news to keep me company.

Old age means giving back
what we had on loan
or maybe that eternal skirmishing
between... *(missing words)...*
None of the seasons knows where
to turn. Butterflies are born
in the east wind's poison
bottle. Even winter's grounded.

What's life but small talk?
We all know what's waiting
                when the fingerpicking's done.
A last chord weeping,
a crowd of people already turned away.

You can lay the blame on my lame imagination

You can lay the blame on my lame imagination
that finds your face in every face along the bar
whether I work at words or glimpse the ghosts that wait in wine.

I've seen you sketched in hills and down the border,
and along the northern roads where every sign
can also blame my lame imagination

for the fiction that says everything is fine
whenever a group of us can get ourselves together
to work on words or glimpse the ghosts that wait in wine.

And in taverns moored up tight to the sea-margin
on a day soon to be famous for sunshine
you can lay the blame on my lame imagination

for provoking you with the usual paranoia
or goading till I've gone beyond the line,
whether I work at words or glimpse the ghosts that wait in wine:

But this morning, with the dew white from its censor,
and this afternoon in every city shrine
you can lay the blame on my lame imagination
for my work of words and the ghosts I glimpse in wine.

The Deluge

It's like a flood, the imagination's fury:
so stubborn it will never yield.

But here in a classroom of children
whose vocabulary's wretched as their council houses

where tenants are swopped as often as Pokemon
cards,
the imagination's a sweet and dirty

red-raw gold, the grain
of a grain you'll spend a fortune to find.

Let's take a picture, I say,
of the streets of this town.

It's a criss-cross, sir,
it's a crossword, yes a crossword,

and the houses and shops are the black squares.
But people are difficult: like words

they mutate as if they were radioactive,
words you can read but never understand.

It's lunch break now and all such words forgotten,
and gold is a game that's hard to play.

The watchman wipes the board
white of his warning.

Outside, the tide
is making up its mind.

Swallows

South, out of the mist
they reveal themselves,
these one, two, these three,

the bow of their swallowtails
hammered straight by sunlight,
their voice radar unearthly,

coming down the modem to us,
their flight patterns
outlining clouds in fine weather,

skirting the ground in rainstorms.
These are meteors that mind
when the sea's moody

and so skirt the margins of the beach,
where the midges are drinking,
or where maggots ferment

in the warmth and the wet.
Now here they come arrowing
themselves like acrobats.

But the only covenant that covers these
is direction's decision,
an unerring aim.

Sunday Morning in New York

It's Easter here, but the churches
that seem to reach for God himself
hold as tightly to their monuments
of all the works of man.

From Staten Island
Manhattan's a safehouse, medieval in its mists,
a precipice of perspex
glittering through the censor's fug.

And if there are any strangers here
under the marble cornice
a priestess of freedom
will ask them to kneel in their innocence

before the glass storefronts
filled with ribboned eggs
and the shiny shopgirls
patrol in tiptoeing politeness.
But when dawn cracks open
its exchequers of light
there's only room for roustabout
out on the avenues

with Broadway lox and bagels
and saxophone music and Samur wine
milling in the memory
when creeping home under the towers.

But at the Whitehorse tap
say a prayer for the damned in the downtown bars,
between Church and Murray,
under the uptown steeples and the Brooklyn stars.

NOTE

Iwan Llwyd was born in 1957 and died suddenly in 2008 aged fifty-two. A lengthy and important discussion of Iwan Llwyd's poetry is *Awen Iwan* (Barddas), 2010. His poetry features in *The Adulterer's Tongue* (2004), Carcanet's collection of poetry in the Welsh language (Cymraeg), in translations by myself. Without Iwan's support the volume would not have been published. He was in favour of translation from the Welsh, when other eminent poets felt it was detrimental to the language.

Iwan's poems in *The Adulterer's Tongue* demonstrate how he embraced north American influences, and revelled in the cultures they suggested and provided. A musician who combined the bass guitar with Welsh language sonnets and the intricate and ancient 'cynghanedd' system of internal poetic sonic harmony, Iwan was as much at home with old, medieval and modern Welsh as he was with The Beatles, Bob Dylan and Leonard Cohen, as seen here in 'Hen Gitar' (Old Guitar).

On one memorable visit from Iwan's home in north- to mine in south Wales, he and I went in search of Bob Dylan's autograph on the wall of 'The Three Golden Cups' pub in Southerndown, near Porthcawl. At the same time, Iwan was writing 'Rhyw Deid yn Dod Miwn', poems about the Welsh coastline, some elements of which I have begun to translate.

As editor of the international magazine *Poetry Wales*, I took Iwan abroad several times (he was the magazine's Welsh language editor), especially to Ireland, Canada, Brazil and the USA. I also arranged for him to perform at Poetry International in London, where he presented poetry in Cymraeg from north Walian schoolchildren. (Note 'The Deluge' here.) I have vivid memories of Iwan explaining to an American poet the complexities of writing an 'englyn', on a napkin on a bar table, during one of the Gerard Manley Hopkins summer schools in Ireland.

Constructing Pavlović

CHRIS MILLER

What premium do you add to the poets you read in translation? Poetry is the hardest taskmaster. A nodding acquaintance with a language may still be a dark glass or a partial view when it comes to reading poetry. For most of us, Osip Mandelstam is not one of those poets whose lines bud in memory at the prompting of event, accessible through their mnemonic perfection, but a dream of a poet, glimpsed through words in which the dream is not fulfilled. For those without Russian, he is the creation as much of our imagination as of what we hear and retain of his words. I want to talk about a poet I have spent half a lifetime hypothesizing and constructing; if I tell you that he is among the essential poets of the twentieth century, my proofs are necessarily lacking. Yet his language is no more untranslatable than that of Zbigniew Herbert or Vasko Popa, whose influence on our own poetry is incontrovertible. He shares with Popa and many others the distinction of writing in a language that no longer exists (and may never have done) and from a country that no longer exists but undoubtedly did. That language was Serbo-Croat, 'which many experts consider as the two separate languages of Serbian and Croatian'.

The poet is Miodrag Pavlović. I first encountered him in the translation published by Angel Books (UK) and New Rivers Press (USA) in 1985: *The Slavs Beneath Parnassus, Selected Poems,* translated by Bernard Johnson. The book was a revelation. Sometimes one reads a poet with the sense that they have been designed for oneself, that their work meets a need previously unknown but as if retrospectively predictable; there ought to have been such a poet, and suddenly it turns out that there is. Many may have had this impression in reading Zbigniew Herbert. The translation conveyed a poet conceptually clean-limbed and swift, whose ideas found just the right correlatives to make a rich symbolic unity of each poem, one that combined satirical modernity with the distancing halo of myth. At the same time, I had the sense that these translations did not fully convey that poet; they gave me to intuit a rhythmic and verbal precision that they did not themselves attain. There is the paradox: Bernard Johnson's translations were at least good enough to give me the idea that they fell short of the original, and my immense gratitude for their existence was tempered by the sense they bewrayed of their own limitations. I was, at all events, sufficiently impressed to write to Bernard, who welcomed my interest and told me that Pavlović would soon be coming to England. I think this must have been in 1985 or 1986.

Pavlović was born in 1928, in Novi Sad, a citizen of the Kingdom of Serbs, Croats and Slovenes, which in 1929 became the Kingdom of Yugoslavia. His first book, *87 Poems* of 1952, was a breakthrough for Serbian or Serbo-Croat modernism (I think Miodrag always thought of himself as writing in Serbian) and coincided with an easing of the cultural Stalinism that had till then prevailed in Tito's breakaway Communist State. The two editions of his *Anthology of Serbian Poetry* proved foundational. He was an essayist, a literary and art critic of national renown, and a kind of ethnologist; he is considered one of the three great poets of his generation, with Ivan V. Lalić and Vasko Popa. Lalić and Popa had a great poet-translator in Francis Jones. Pavlović was not quite so lucky; Bernard Johnson, Lecturer in Russian at the LSE and a specialist in Serbo-Croat, was formidably expert but not, perhaps, as gifted a translator of poetry – not, at least, till the translations of Jovan Hristić that he published at the very end of his life. In Canada, Barry Callaghan published two English-Serbian parallel texts, one his translation of a single volume, the other (I think) a translation of a French selection. I encountered these somewhat later and have failed to make contact with Callaghan for the purposes of this essay; I cannot therefore say whether he was translating with Pavlović from the Serbian or from French with the assistance of Pavlović's French translator (whom Callaghan also translated). For in French, Pavlović had a splendid ally, his friend and 'brother' Robert Marteau, poet, novelist, essayist and alchemist. Marteau had no Serbian but worked directly with the author: 'I made those translations like a blind man with his stick, if you lead him astray, he falls; I touched every syllable with my stick... I tremble at the thought of it, translation is something terrible, terrible.' He nevertheless translated a selected and two individual volumes. Finally, Mireille Robin translated a much broader selection than Marteau's for the French publisher Circe in 2008. A more recent Selected Poems, co-translated into English by the poet James Sutherland-Smith and his colleague Nenad Aleksić, seems to have been slightly hampered by Pavlović's choices of poem; fragmentary extracts from longer poems make little sense and the poet was anxious that he should not again be represented in English by his 'greatest hits'. There are a number of translations into German but they are, alas, inaccessible to me.

Cross-referencing is therefore the order of the day. Pavlović's most translatable work comes in a series of volumes constituting a single span: *The Milk of Origins* (1963), *Great Scythia* (1969), *New Scythia* (1970), *Sacrificial Procession* (1971) and *Light and Dark Holidays* (1971). In the first, classical civilisation is evoked as a succession of dying orders, from the dogs of Knossos greeting the Dorian invaders to the late Archaic poet Pindar lamenting the death of his culture shortly before the dawn of the classical period. The ancient Greeks do not represent, as they do in Seferis, some distant ideal barely remembered in the decadent civilisation of today, but rather rehearse in their own epoch the failures of today's world. *Great Scythia* is concerned with 'the ambience of South Slav prehistory, the confrontation of a primitive, dynamic, pagan society with the remains of a great civilisation that it supersedes'; in *New Scythia,* Pavlović goes on to evoke Byzantine and Serbian history and the inevitable 'Field of Kosovo', the scene of Serbia's mythological martyrdom (in 1389, Prince Lazar confronted Sultan Murad I and was killed in a battle that effectively ended Serbian Christian resistance to the Ottoman Empire). In *Holidays,* the Christian festivals and their Serbian traditions are used to reflect more widely on the roles of religion and ritual in human life.

The key to Pavlović's fascination as a poet is, perhaps, his attitude to myth. Johnson describes him as fascinated by the 'development [of universal myths] from semi-historical, semi-traditional sources'; 'Great events, famous men and heroic deeds become hallowed by the myths that grow up around them, and it is these myths, overlaid by generations of folk, traditional and religious layers of adaptation and belief, that the poet sees as vast repositories of mankind's collective experience'. This influenced him as both poet and critic. In his *Anthology of Serbian Poetry*, he selected poems that, he said, spoke about 'the fundamental questions of individual and collective existence, poems that either convey a thought or lead through their content directly to cognition'. Well, as you see, translation is not simply an issue for poetry. And Pavlović's words somewhat predate the hermeneutics of suspicion, a point doubly paradoxical since, in the Eastern and Central European socialist states, the very word 'truth' *(pravda)* was synonymous with propaganda.

Pavlović's poems thus lay claim to a kind of archetypal status; they offer a kind of philosophical parable. This is obviously akin to the Aesopian style that many Eastern European poets shared; it is not, I would argue, quite the same thing. A poem such as Zbigniew Herbert's 'To Marcus Aurelius' implies that the waves of barbarians threatening the Pax Romana are close kin to the northern barbarians then occupying Poland; the Stoic is seen at once as exemplary emperor and exemplary philosopher. The two forms of order, political and philosophical, that he represents have been simultaneously destroyed and what is left is a kind of dystopian horror. In 'Drawer', Herbert regrets the integrity that his poems have lost by being published and earning money and reputation; the dialectic described is universal but takes much of its poignancy from the compromised public positions of recognised poets in Soviet states, where a kind of unofficial dissidence might be a price that the state was prepared to pay in order to insist that its artists and authors were free, while the official authors were well-rewarded for a loyalty that they either brazenly expressed or took care not to reject outright. This is not intended as a criticism of Herbert, who can undoubtedly lay claim to the creation of philosophical parables. But it was the nature of many of those parallels that they often spoke of what was forbidden and did so in Aesopian ways. These were problems that Pavlović did not have to contend with so directly. There were topics that could not be raised in Tito's Yugoslavia during the 1960s and 1970s, but they were often – by no means always – remote from Pavlović's concerns

A part of his distinction as a poet might be said to arise from Serbia's lack of pre-Communist industrial development and urbanisation. Folkloric language and national myth are or were close to the surface in Serbia, where Albert Lord went to find oral bards still improvising long poems to the rhythms of the guslar in the manner of the Homeric bards. The myth of Kosovo Field is still resonant. The past is peculiarly alive in Serbia as it is in Poland; the Ottomans attempted to extinguish Serbian identity as the occupying powers attempted to extinguish the Polish nation. Both countries see themselves as martyrs whose suffering is owed to their position on the battlefront of East and West, and these attitudes are thoroughly enrooted in popular sentiment. When the West comes criticising, both countries are liable to revive a martyr complex. Pavlović was therefore able to enrich an essentially modern discourse by the use of folkloric language, with its epic connotations. And he had no low opinion of the role of the poet, whom he saw as a shaman, at once alien and essential to *les mots de la tribu*. Here is one of his outcast shamans, in a version translated from Marteau's French:

The Traveller Departs

First light.
Church bells not yet woken.
The very spring-water is still.

I'm leaving.
No one likes me in Church or town,
Not even my family.

I walk over the shoulder of the mountain.
Ancient sunlight climbs through the pines,
Alights on my lips.

From high up, a robe of smoke descends;
Another angel brought down.

An earthenware plate in my pack, I stride out,
The listening in me spreads out
(Shells whispering in the flesh);
Silence carries me off on its broad-backed river.

But I shall come back to this place
To tell them the true name of the smoke
And the new name for the sun.

It can immediately be seen that Pavlović's is a pared-back art and occasionally obscure. Marteau's French implies that the angel has been shot down, while the line about 'shells' translates Marteau's 'conques partout dans la chair' ('conches everywhere in the flesh'), which seems a surprising apposition to the notion of *ouïe* (hearing); conches are better known for their ritual blaring. Part of the problem of 'reconstructing' the poet and the poem in translation is that one cannot know why one connotation was preferred to another in the process of translation. Nevertheless, the poem has – at least in French – a superlatively archetypal quality; the poet's alienation from the tribe is in the nature of his condition, and he (mostly, in these archetypes, 'he') must leave behind the society into which he was born, like Thomas Mann's Tonio Kröger. He will return with his vision accomplished, and his poems will change the way even 'chambermaids speak', as Mário Antonio (reinforcing the sexism of the archetype) said of Pessoa's work.

The burden of *Great Scythia* is the transition between classical culture and the new culture made on its ruins by the barbarian invaders from the steppes; they thrill to the destruction that they have caused, then look around them in wonder at what they have destroyed. Here Pavlović reminds me of Herbert's poem 'Longobards', in which the barbarians from the frozen north, the Germanic tribes who gave their name to Lombardy, arrive with their slogan 'nothingnothingnothing'. But Pavlović is more hopeful, as befits a poet from a culture that is mythically heir to the Scythian riders – a people whose nomadic civilisation seemed so very barbarian to the sedentarised urban populations. This is one of Pavlović's greatest poems, marvellously rendered in French by Marteau, somewhat less satisfactory in Bernard Johnson's English. So I have again attempted my own impertinent reconstruction, plundering part of Bernard's wording:

The Slavs Beneath Parnassus

Our chiefs led us to these Southern lands,
Drunk on unbelief, green with vigour
To bite the marble flanks
Break down the mountains
With our clubbing blows,
Drive the terror-stricken flocks into the sea.
Here in the blue we dance our wild dances
And sleep naked among the shattered idols.

But our singers whisper questions in our ear:
Who attended the funeral of the sky,
Who witnessed the death-throes of eternity?
And they said: we should spend the nights
Not in destruction but in song.
At dawn the great ships will approach
Bearing the beautiful lords of the land
And set anchor on the mountain top.
The divine will arise with the dawn;
Hands will descend on our shoulders
And bless us as their newfound sons.

Then our nakedness will be covered with words
As birches clothe themselves with leaves in Spring.

The poem positions the Slavs not just as the barbarians who destroyed a culture but as those who inherited its mantle. And in any culture, the forgotten gods remain, as quotidian as the days of the week. Who remembers the Norse god of war, Tyr? He is more obscure than the Roman god that he replaced in the English weekday, the Mars of *mardi* or *martes* or *martedì*. Such a deity is the burden of another masterly poem, 'Svetovid Speaks'. Svetovid or Svetovit was the *deus deorum* of the West Slavs and his stronghold was Arkona on the German island of Rügen, which is perhaps most famous for the Romantic sublime of Caspar David Friedrich and the Nazi seaside resort of Prora. He had four heads and was represented by an eight-metre wooden statue. Arkona was captured when Christianisation was enforced by Valdemar I of Denmark. The relation of Svetovid to Serbia passes through his association with St. Vitus (their Serbian names are nearly homophonic); the battle of Kosovo Field was fought on the feast day of Vitus.

Svetovid Speaks

The wounds of decapitation are still stinging.
My four severed heads on the sea-floor
Mumble Slavonic words even now.

A conspiracy woven from Bethlehem
To the Balkans! A migrant
Faith hastened south, then
Battened on us, sword in hand; I, its victim.

I, a divinity. I'm a monster now.
In the transmutation of stone and man,
I fell behind. Now my blond children
Chant the praise of some other deity.

Even plants have longer lives than the gods.
Humans embrace a hope
Of afterlife. No afterlife for me.

In servitude, in battle, no one now
Calls on the name of the forgotten idol.

Bitter is the fate of the gods and their bitter attachment
To the human race that wantonly changes odour and
faith.

Only the beekeepers remain to nurture
Their honey in the trunk of my tongue.

I have said that Pavlović was not Aesopian, and had little need to be. But this could hardly be altogether true of a poet working in a Communist republic, and his account of the Second Coming reflects rambunctiously on the supposed new millennium of Communism, with its 'voluntary' duties like the curation of the neighbourhood in the comrade citizen's spare time (or like litter-picking duties in an English public school). This version is concocted from Bernard's English and Mireille Robin's French.

The Poet Rises from the Ground

The winds blew through the earth and the molehills,
Deeper than any plough or probe,
The strata of the sounds began to swell beneath us,
And the kernel of music was rent in twain.
Against the blue sky, I saw outlined
My own body with the head of a cat,
While my real head was here at my armpit.

Then they threw nets over us – nets full of moonshine
And electric shocks, they dragged us, we dead,
To the surface of the earth, whipped us on our feet
While we were still too numb to move; it's not easy
To take on the mould of some new form.

They needed to wake us, they filled us too full
With energy, glowing like filaments

We trod the fields of the early dawn;
While we were marching, they managed to combine
Our heads, our faces, our limbs, our bodies, then
They stuck flowers in our hands, heavens above! –
As though we were a bunch of gays, not the resurrected,
And all that for someone else's sake.

So! The resurrection of the dead was no myth, after
all!
We shake off the congealed mud and wait for the
review.
We're hoping some of us can go now, each to their
own,
Meeting the family or taking a walk. No such luck!
The angels turn up with hot water and brushes: 'Get
on!
Clean up the mountains and the valleys! Purify the way
Of the Lord who called you back into this life!'

So, after all, it's just like the army; I've become a lackey
again,
Whereas, when I was dead, I was a perfect dissident,
No could ever make me do anything. Which is why
I was hoping for some honour, some literary prize,
When the archangel summoned me by name!

It is probably clear that the speaker of the poem, at least, is homophobic, and the term 'gay' insufficiently pejorative to suit his discourse. Does it also go without saying that the term 'dissident' is anachronistic, a translator's grace note or distortion? Pavlović was no dissident, at least to the extent that he was widely published, and a form of cultural export; sometimes, success abroad could defend the Soviet poet at home, where the show of a little free speech could only speak well of the totalitarian state from which it came. The term 'dissident' inevitably leads us to a clearly Aesopian poem, no doubt set in the Byzantine Empire, where the Nestorians, a Christian sect, preferred the tolerant rule of Islam to the carnivorous theological zealotry of Byzantium. This is translated from the French of Mireille Robin.

A Provincial Governor Complains about the Heretics

What do these lunatics want?
What's all the fuss about?
As if our earthly empire could be improved!
In vain they plague me, I don't want to crack down,
But these people, always asking for *more* justice,
Keep me awake at night and drive me bonkers.

Insolent weaklings, they look contrite when they talk
to me,
Then go down to the main square and shout their
heads off.
Why do they want to turn our jovial credo
Into something painful and joyless? No form of
beauty
Meets *their* approval. They convince everyone
They're on the wrong road – but catch *them* repenting...

They've made me lose my rag, these villains,
They cling to me like flesh-eating bugs in a tomb!
Others would have their throats cut,
Burn them alive on pyres or mill their bones.
I prefer more radical solutions: I cool their ardour
With a stone to the head, I say: 'Too much blood has
flowed!
Off to bed with you now, zip-zap: sleep!'

But the inconvenient dead seem less than sleepy;
They shower houses with a reddish water, and while
The guards lead them to some quarry outside the
gates,
Bloody mucus flows off the roofs, then the leafage
Of trees hung with their bodies reddens like autumn:
Damnable magic tricks – that proves they were guilty!

I have really horrid dreams, with birds pecking their
veins,
Their red trunks rise from the river-water like toads,
Above them a black-bearded man with a violin
announces:
This is my brother, in whom I am well pleased.

Nobody ever talks to me like that! Why am *I* being
mocked?
They send me the worst of the rabble, then say, 'But
He was a man of justice', wanting to know why I
punished them,
If they go on like this, I shall lose the Emperor's
favour!

You can always justify heretics, especially the dead
ones,
But what about me? I have to sort out the palace
plots!
I have to live with the fearful anger of the Lord!

Mention of Byzantium brings me to a poem that comes closer to the category of philosophical parable. There is surely some aspect of everyone's life with which this poem resonates. It is cobbled together from Bernard's English and Mireille Robin's French.

The Returned Pilgrim

I came to the immemorial city
To discover the icons and psalters of ritual joy
To sing with the choir under the golden arches.
The Varangian guard tried to keep me out,
No communion for the likes of me at Hagia Sofia:
I walked the streets thirsting (which is why
I drink a lot of wine these days);
I was miserable that I could not give alms to the beggars
Though I was not a beggar myself. In this city
Of ships and flowers, I knew no one
But the Good Lord Himself.
I slept on the straw among the horses,
Vied with the sweet voices of the Armenians in the stables,
And at the week's end, when the moon was young,
I fled, empty-handed, back to our forested land
And its profusion of game. But once I was back,
On a mountain with a name you could never pronounce,

I felt nostalgic for the city and its port crowned with gold.
It seemed I could see them every morning through the mist,
The distant continents bound together by their radiance.
And now, as I age under my sheepskin cloak,
I know that wandering, lonely and impoverished,
Through the streets of the capital of the universe
Was the closest I came to the beauty of this world.

I met Miodrag through Bernard those many years ago, and through Miodrag, I made friends with Robert Marteau. I owe Miodrag a debt, because I tried, when he was in England, to promote him. It was not a success. He was at least paid for the reading he gave at the Oxford Union, which was attended by Bernard, myself, one other organiser, and, fortunately, by some of the family of the poet who had agreed to read the English translation, Robert Crawford. Posters bearing Miodrag's name failed to attract crowds to his reading, because his name was unknown. 'Leading Yugoslav Poet' would probably have had the same effect. I tried to interview him by post in the days before email but failed, partly because all that I knew about him at the time was contained in Bernard's introduction; I effectively had to ask him what questions I should put. This essay is intended as an *amende honorable*, in the hope that a translator of real poetic skill and some direct connection with Serbian might offer us an English Pavlović of distinction.

Outfitters

TOM PICKARD

February 20th

The house was in chaos, but we talked.

'You'll never find your way back. I mean, how could you? Ever?'

One of the girls on the bed took off her bra and we embraced.

'Can I stay and sleep for a while, I'm tired?'

February 25th

Foggy. Light wind and drizzle. The café, silent – which means, when they close (for the rest of the week), the lasses will bring me the unsold food that hasn't passed its sell-by date. At mid-afternoon there's a shuffling of seats and a few cheerful voices are audible through the partition between the café and my room, against which I've built a floor to ceiling bookcase to reduce the sound.

To allay cage fever I walked into a thick roak, to photograph anything that aspired to an outline, and heard a biker accelerate into oblivion's foggy masticating maw.

February 26th

As we stood on a balcony, she laid her warm cheek against my neck.

'I wish you wouldn't move away from here.'

As though her *here* were her. I turned aside, sorrowful, 'it's difficult'.

The Velux windows that face each other, west to east, are slightly open and an icy northeaster, on a long leash down from the Arctic, snaps, howls and lurches through powerlines with fast pugnacious gusts that hit the floor and shake it.

'They took him to the hospital, and the nurse came oot and said to the lad who was waiting, you might as well get yourself a cup of coffee because as soon as Eric seen the needle he fainted.'

'Load of fucking shite.'

'He's got three stitches in his brow; you can see the scar, and the nurse said she'd take them oot. These two lads had to take him there.'

'Aye, we took him to see the nurse…'

'You fucking bastard…'

'… and as she was taking the stitches oot…'

'Your knuckles were white.'

'… one dropped doon her front.'

'And when we came oot he said, *she's hardly got owt on, under that pinny…*'

'There wasn't a stitch on her.'

'Aye, and while the wound was open he was trying to get his Krugerrand in, before it was stitched up.'

'Don't say anything about his Krugerrand, on the tape, mind.'

February 28th

Last night I drove across the North Pennines to Reeth, in North Yorkshire, to see Kathryn Tickell and Corrina Hewat's final gig of their tour. Kathryn used a photo of mine for the cover of their new cd – cotton grass blowing a kiss to low cloud. When the gig was over, we sat at a fireside table in the Black Cock and downed a few drinks. Kathryn's mother had driven over for the gig from Croglin, which is situated a few miles below me, in the Eden Valley, and is home to a Vampire legend. She was, like the rest of us, staying overnight in the pub. Jigs from the gig were jingling in my ear, the beer and the company were good and I was in my tops, which is when Mrs Tickell asked how was life on the hill, and I told her; fine.

'That lad who broke his tooth the other night, can he charge for his dental treatment?'

'A pipe swung back and knocked the lad's teeth out. I forgot what their argument was, but we couldn't claim.'

'Jim the riveter says to Joe the Duck, when he was heating rivets, he says '*at twenty to twelve [h]'eat them two pies up for me, will you?*' Joe ate them.'

'Four letters, in the crossword, sorry three letters, *part of the ear.* Lug. I'm not kidding you, lug.'

'The new managing director come in and made a speech; spoke to us as though we were school kids. He turned round to Carty and says, *well, what do you want to say about that then?* And Carty just laughed.'

'He's got a fucking good vocabulary.'

'When the MD finished, he said, *any comments?* And Carty says, *we've had these lion-tamers coming in here before, big blokes with the big boots on.'*

'The Personnel Director used to say *don't upset the MD, he's a bad bugger.*'

'Aye and Carty would say *fuck off, fuck him.'*

'They were shitting themselves.'

'How did you end up in a place like that?' Asked Mrs Tickell.

'It was July and the cotton grass was out, the skies were high and studded with lark song and echoing curlews; snipes were drumming, wild thyme and mountain primroses underfoot, the heather coming into bloom.'

'No, but really?'

My third marriage broke up and I had nowhere to go. The accommodation in the café was the cheapest I could find on Alston Moor and that's where I wanted to be. I've always yearned to live in wilderness. At the age of ten I developed an affection for an ancient sycamore that the Blakelaw kids called 'the old four legged'. We didn't talk to it or hug it, other than to cling on as we scrambled up its trunk and perched in the fork of high branches to get thrown about in a strong wind. But I didn't tell her that.

'I shudder when I drive over that pass and the café is hidden from sight,' said Mrs Tickell.

'My island in the clouds.'

'Like a Prospero, said Kathryn.'

'More of a Caliban.'

'Don't you worry about burglars?'

'I keep a log-splitter by the door, and an axe by the bed.'

'What about when you're away from home, like tonight?'

'I leave a twenty quid note on the table, as part compensation to the scally for screwing my impoverished gaff.'

'So, your insurance is a twenty-pound tip for the burglars?' asked Mrs Tickell.

'Yes, in the hope they won't trash the place.'

'Maybe they'll tidy it up,' said Kathryn.

When I have to be away from home I could leave everything where it is and hope the gaff won't be burgled, or, which is what I've taught myself to do when leaving for more than a couple of days, pack my tools into boxes and bags, drive them down to Alston and along the South Tyne valley to Station House in Lamely where my friends Joyce and Graham Smith give them house room.

When unable to stash my gear at Station House, my only option is to crawl through to the adjoining, equally un-insulated, attic – which is directly over the café and has its share of dusty loft-junk as well as a couple of water tanks which are fed from a spring on the fell by a pump which sometimes develops a splutter and gives up altogether – and hide in there forty years of letters from friends, poets, family; my tools – stereo, pc, Dat recorder, video camera, still camera, lenses, microphones – all items that are essential for the job and which I would never have the money to replace if stolen. Then the media those tools generate, which includes a few hundred hours of video and audio conversations with workers from a shipyard in Sunderland (50 miles away on the river Wear, which has its headwaters leaking from a bog near here), that Thatcher was shutting down to build yuppie flats over; hours of winds recorded on the fells through gaps in dykes, through whistling gates, though dried reeds, through heather, from behind a rock with song ripped from larks in the midst of gales; recordings of a Celtic harp dragged to a high point where winds from different directions met, blew together and played it.

'Why not leave a recording of rottweilers barking?' Kathryn suggested.

'I'm planning to leave a tape of ferocious winds, running on a continuous loop.'

'But what if it's calm outside when the burglars listen at the window?'

'They'd hear a man-eating tempest raging inside my gaff.'

'It would confuse me', she said, 'the world inside out.'

'Inside the outside-world, inside.'

But my shipyard tapes, recorded in the mid eighties, work better. Those from bait-huts and shop stewards' offices break into rowdy banter when someone is wound-up, or slapped down, until they squeal, followed by a meltdown of loud laughter from his tormentors. And after a short period of silence someone's knackers are twitched in another cruel twist and the wind-up rewinds.

'I'll tell you what, Tom, when you write your book, if you ever want any war stories or owt like that, Eddy is your boy.'

'Or if you ever want to know anything about sharks.'

'... King Farouk, Queen Fareda...'

'I don't know what you want to read into this, but he was the camp plumber in the war.'

Ronnie starts to whistle quietly to himself, gazing into a corner.

'And you obviously know that Ronnie is a retired singer? A choirboy.'

'Oh, aye, me? Without a doubt.' He starts to hum. 'You're going back forty years.'

'In these three shop stewards' offices, there's some fucking talent, like. We've got a guy here beat Sebastian Coe, running...'

'I heard about him.'

'Who?'

'The rabbit.'

'Especially if he sees his mate in a fight.'

'He's the type of bloke, who, if you were under fire in a battle, would volunteer to gan and get the ammunition but wouldn't come back.'

'Eh'?

'His theme song is *'run rabbit run rabbit run, run, run'*.

'So would you if there was fucking twenty of the cunts.'

'Aye, but you left your fucking mate getting scagged'

'They were black-and-white bastards'. (Turns to Pickard) 'No offence'.

Mrs Tickell nodded down towards the large bags and bulging backpack that I had tucked in under the table.

'That's a hell of a lot of luggage for an overnight stay, Tom'.

They were stacked with shipyard tapes, notebooks I hadn't transcribed, and not just those put together since moving to Hartside, but from a lifetime – the earliest dating back to when I was thirteen in the shape of a small Letts schoolboy diary that notes the day our first telly would arrive, and has a list of girls tucked away at the back before the weights and measures and times-tables – a lifetime of scribblyjacking packed into a few dozen notebooks of various sizes.

It's a working archive: four decades of sharpening tools, of false starts, of half abandoned shots, of research on a few dozen projects with notes from and of primary sources, witness statements, dream journals: sacks of mistakes to ditch and burn if they don't alchemically transmute into art which they might if I'm long enough in one place to unpack. None have been digitised, otherwise my load would be lighter: and I do know that a load of used paper is just what a housebreaker seeks. The Ode Thief, The Great Haiku Heist, The Villanelle Villainies, The Stolen Sonnets, A Swag Bag of Blagged Ballads by Border Badlads, a handful of Housebreaker's Heroic Couplets, Nocked-off Nocturns.

'Why don't you read us an extract from one of your journals?' Said Mrs Tickell.

'No fucking way.'

'Oh, go on, Tom', urged Kathryn.

When walking the fells I make an attempt at an always-on language, trying to find and describe what's happening inside and out, and to get as close as I dare to my demons. It's an experiment and open to chance that a form will emerge. Sometimes truth becomes the slut of fancy and I follow where it takes me. One of my nicknames at school was *taxi-door lugs,* always open: a lifelong snaffler-up of trinkets. At risk of sounding folksy, I spent my childhood listening to old Katie McKenna, who had a long memory for family histories that were sometimes tragic or brutal: and that fed into my early poems.

'at thirteen I failed to become
a complete teddy boy
owing to my mother's dark memories
of Mosley mobs
she did not buy me a black shirt' [from 'Hero Dust']

She told me uncle Adam was squashed to death in the railways yards and I retold it.

My father was a railway man
And there he got stuck
Squashed between the buffers
Of two shunting trucks

The next verse is about her.

Mother was a charwife
used to char for you
Kept your hands lily-white
Hers needed seeing to
She scrubbed your stairs
And scrubbed your floors
Peeled her hands with Flash
While you were having manicures
Riding on her back
[from What Can You Do?]

She had a fiercely intuitive, non-doctrinaire radicalism, and always voted – even if it was a bit like filling in a betting slip for Billy, the illicit booky. After a few years of Thatcher's free market butchery of the north, Katie, in her eighties, would say *'if I had a gun, I would shoot her'*. And I often heard old ladies of her generation in the toon say the same thing to anyone within earshot. It was an active mantra in the bingo halls and on the busses going home.

In 1966 Stuart Montgomery sent me Edward Dorn's 'Geography', which he'd recently published with Fulcrum Press. Dorn had just started teaching at Essex University – a job set up for him by Donald Davie. I wrote and told him how much I liked the book and would he do a gig in the Morden Tower, which he did. He wrote to Charles Olson of his visit, describing our flat in Newcastle *'one morning I woke up at his place and it was so damn cold I shook till my eyes finally opened, for the first time in too long I realized, I suddenly felt wide awake...'* He would have felt wide awake here, too, on Fiends Fell some forty years later. When I complained to him about feeling hopeless and impotent against the system he said, 'well, just be a witness'. So, these journals are also that, even if all that is witnessed is a change of light. They're a refuge, a place to put anything and everything – in an order of chance occurrence: the chronology of 'incident' is irrelevant even if, at the same time, essential. It's where I keep myself company; a place to wander off track into the unknown, to become lost in a whiteout and sink up to the neck in bog. A place to play and be played. *'The Dark Months of May'* is being cherry-picked from these journals: *'The Ballad of Jamie Allan'* is taking shape in them. Everything I have is in them. They're what I'd grab first in a fire – it's what I was and who I am or who I might be, at least to myself.

He brought Ezekiel's baggage. Hannah opened it, and on top she found a bundle of long sheets of paper, carefully wrapped. They were covered in verse in Hebrew, and Abram was the only one of them who could read it all. Ezekiel had been somewhat free in his speech, and Hannah was afraid there might be something Nihilistic in his writing that would get them all into trouble. She was afraid to ask an outsider what the writing was about. In those days it was enough to say of a family, 'they are Nihilists,' to have them arrested at once; the police investigated at their leisure. There was too much to burn at one time, so she burnt a few sheets every morning until they were gone. As she put the first into the fire she said, 'Here's a man's life'[13]

'What do you write in your notebooks, Tom?' Mrs Tickell persisted.

'Life on the fells, the weather, the birds, the winds, the sound of watta, and folks' natta, dreams, everything and anything – ravens and raves – it's a place to think and reflect, observe and play – like gulls and crows in the wind over a clough on the fells, returning over and over to the thrust-up gusts that propels them, like kids down a slide on ice.'

'Oh, well, you must let us hear something now', said Mrs Tickell.

'Not a chance', I replied, and swallowed the best part of a pint and got up to get another.

When I returned with a round, she said:

'You're such a tease. Why don't you take any notebook at random, open it anywhere and read it to us?'

There was a warm fire murmuring, and the jigs were still reeling in my ears and I was sufficiently drunk to take the gamble. If I hadn't tippled from bliss to blitzed with that last drink I could have improvised some salacious mischief, or, Scheherazade-like, a made-up dream of seduction to get them pink and perhaps a little breathless. I pulled out from under the table one of the bags between my legs and blind, like Justice as a Bingo caller, grabbed a black-bound notebook, flipped it open wherever it would, and jacked myself to read some stormy ramble over broken hills, some lyric poem:

'13th of June. London. Blew me giro on a bevvy last night and I'm skint. Got up at 6 and caught the first train north, from Kings Cross.'

13 Charles Reznikoff's 1930 novel, *By The Waters of Manhattan.*

The Sinai Lepoard and other poems

CHRISTOPHER RIESCO

The Sinai Leopard

In a low-rate hotel, the fool sipped on a little black bottle. It was supposed to be magic. He remembered seeing a boy and a girl, when he was a boy. Suddenly they appeared in the room. Their skin was like icing-sugar. The next night, he took another sip, intending to make the most of his collection of memories – but a memory came to him unbidden, of the time when he saw a Sinai Leopard. It was big and heavy. It bared its teeth. The bottle fell out of his hand, and its contents spilled on the carpet.

The Flyswat

The playa was endless,
like the shift he was working. The little hut
with its row of beer pumps and its blackboard
of prices was full of flies, and sometimes
he would try to hit them with the electric flyswat
but that game lost its fun after the first few kills.
Round men with red faces and their shirts open
queued up for their plastic pint glasses of beer.
They went for Stella. Always Stella. They blinked.
He felt his shirt stick to his back with sweat.

Días Perdidos

From the turret, you can see out
across the flat, featureless water,
and if you put a coin in the public telescope
you can see a grey blur that might be
Morocco. There is one Moroccan export
the girls are quite keen on. Adela carefully
rolls up a joint on the coffee-table, like a jeweller.
The others wait, respectfully.

Flying Ant Season

On the way to the shop, and back, I see fat, angry, red-faced people,
arguing and slapping flying ants off themselves.

They're like knock-off wasps but with a bit more mystique
because you hardly see them. Except for a few days like today.
One of them lands on my left arm.
The sensation is scraping, itchy, metallic maybe, inquisitive.

I walk along and let my fair-weather friend hitch a lift.
At my door I gently shake it off.

Who Are You?*

Once, in an angular concrete hotel in Antibes,
you stood before the black curtain
with the massive sunlight on the other side
and a heartbeat in your chest.
You reached up, then dropped your hands.
You tapped your hands on your naked hips.
You reached up again and pulled the curtains wide.
You looked several stories down
on an empty round swimming pool
in a square of concrete
surrounded by vacant recliners.
The city grumbled in the background.
There was no one to see you.
You thought for a while,
then got dressed, and joined
your family for breakfast.

Now you're older, and it's traditional.
You undress smoothly, then drag
the curtains open briskly, and look down
inquiringly on the scene below.
Different hotel, different swimming pool,
different recliners.
These ones have people on them.
You study them like a seasoned pro.
The hotel is called the Hotel Hurricane
and the pool is surrounded by tall palm trees.
The window you appear in is arched, Moorish.

Some people are in the opposite role,
always on a recliner, looking up at glass.
Chancers. Because you never know.
The figure who never appeared
in one hotel might be waiting in another.
In Tarifa, perhaps?

You are such a person.
Look to your right and left.
The innocent are snoring,
mouths open in the sun.
You scan the windows.

Some of us are on the desk, always,
next to a bowl of complimentary mints, and the people
who pass through pay more attention to the mints.
Our suits are polyester. We might be
from one of the old families of Jaffa,
and you wouldn't know.

In Palma where the avenues are flat and wide
and the tiled roofs and wiry trees
catch the light and the breeze off the sea
it is easy to have two jobs, teaching
Yoga one day, volleyball the next.
Your neighbourhood is called Gentilico.
Your lessons take place on the beach
called Playa Ciudad Jardín.
Your teaching pays for you to sit in a blue kaftan
on the balcony of your house, with one of your proteges
giving you head, grateful for your hand in their hair.

Or you could always be one of those people
who stands outside a particular house in the evening,
and one of the residents walks out to meet you,
and gives you paper money, and you pass them
a little bag and walk away calmly. You're in direct
sight of the customs office and you don't care.
From the little ferry port below, the white ships pass
from Lemnos to Samothrace and Mytilene.

* *poem originally appeared here: https://thewritelaunch.com/2022/09/who-are-you/*

A Real Piece of Work

It's refreshingly dark and cool.
Ships stand in illuminated glass cases.
You study the standing and the running
rigging of galleons and caravels
and frigates and clippers and xebecs.
Square sails. Lateen sails.
You can follow the lines with your eye but it makes no sense.
You're happily bemused.

There's a room with old wooden figureheads
looming forward in bright colours. A dolphin. A Turk. Nuestra Señorita.
A tiger. John the Baptist. There is an old man wandering in that room,
eyeing the figureheads with a hostile squint,
chewing and muttering. You wonder
if maybe he's become detached from his family.
Could he have dementia? It's as if he's taking the figureheads
for real people, who are having a laugh with him.
The figureheads stare back at him with big painted eyes and painted smiles.
Then he turns to you and says 'A real piece of work'.

Throwaway Song

The smoky lamb is on the skewer.
The drains are backed up to the sewer.

The pines are still, in high July.
And as for sherry, sherry's dry,

but the most particular smell in the world
is the same perfume on a different girl.

A Honeycomb

You can't mistake the heap of freshened earth,
or the oblong box, that rolls into the hearth.
You know a birthday party, anyone's.
You hear the buzz around a honeycomb.

'Make it scotch and dirty river water'

Richard Hugo and James Wright

TONY ROBERTS

They were old friends, driven by insecurities to depression and drink. They had grown up, in Hugo's phrase, in 'poor, often degrading circumstances' during the Depression, with 'loyalty to defeated people' they loved and did not want to be like. They shared 'a feeling of having violated' their lives 'by wanting to be different'. War and education enabled them to escape from home – Hugo's in White Center, Washington State, Wright's in Martins Ferry, Ohio – but memory always brought them back. Their work is marked by a loneliness which seeks identification and acceptance, by a fascination with the rejected (Wright) and the derelict (Hugo). And yet they wrote with a liveliness of style and a candour that is magnetic.

Wright has the greater reputation. He is the more startling, the more varied, the more technically gifted: *The Branch Will Not Break* (1963); *Shall We Gather at the River* (1967); his *Collected Poems* (1971) which won a Pulitzer Prize. Hugo's best work is to be found in *Death of the Kapowsin Tavern* (1965) and *The Lady in Kicking Horse Reservoir* (1973). His posthumously collected poems, *Making Certain It Goes On*, appeared in 1984.

The two met in Theodore Roethke's class at the University of Montana in the mid-1950s. Roethke, another poet beset by personal difficulties, proved a powerful teacher. In his essay 'Stray Thoughts on Roethke and Teaching' Hugo reckoned Roethke's great strength was that he 'gave students a love of the sound of language': 'He was also playful in class, arrogant, hostile, tender, aggressive, receptive – anything that might work to bring the best out of a student'. Wright 'adopted many of Roethke's methods and modelled his own rapport with students after Roethke's presence in the classroom', according to his biographer, Jonathan Blunk (*James Wright: A Life in Poetry*, 2017). Wright reckoned that 'A course with Roethke was a course in very, very detailed and strenuous critical reading'. Caroline Kizer – with David Wagoner another alumnus of this group – remembered Roethke's influence in 'rigorous revision', though the class itself was 'a nest of singing chauvinists'.

Richard Hugo (born 1923) came from a poor Seattle suburb, 'whose reputation for violence and wild behaviour seemed to put it at the edge of civilization', he wrote. He lived with strict, uncommunicative grandparents. Softball and fishing became his 'simple compensations'. During the war he served as a bombardier in the Army Air Corps in the Mediterranean. Subsequently he took two degrees at the University of Washington, and married in 1952. Although employed by the Boeing Company in Seattle as a technical writer, he and his wife lived improvidently and shabbily, by his own account.

Hugo always had difficulty in his relationships with the opposite sex and the guilt, which he wrote openly about later, intensified when his first wife left him:

Lawns well trimmed remind you of the train
your wife took one day forever, some far empty town,
the odd name you never recall. The time: 6:23.
The day: October 9. The year remains a blur.
'What Thou Lovest Well Remains American'

He finally published *A Run of Jacks* with the University of Minnesota Press in 1961, took a year in Italy and became a visiting lecturer at the University of Montana in 1964, the year his wife left him. The title poem of *The Lady in Kicking Horse Reservoir* he disconcertingly described as being 'as close to direct vengeance as I'd come':

Not my hands but green across you now.
Green tons hold you down, and ten bass curve
teasing in your hair.

Hugo's defensive misogynism ended with a stabilizing second marriage in 1974. He was to remain at Montana, later as head of their creative writing programme. Afflicted by health problems in later life, he claimed that he stopped drinking: 'I began to see that a lot of my grief was old and shopworn and only the booze had kept it alive.' However, celebrity made abstinence difficult.

James Wright was born four years later than Hugo, his hometown a rail hub and river port with a population of sixteen thousand. While he claimed 'a peculiar kind of devotion' to Martins Ferry and the Ohio Valley, he wrote privately of it as an 'unspeakable rat-hole'. His father worked at the Hazel-Atlas Glass Company, his mother in a laundry. The town compounded Wright's personal unhappiness. He saw it as a place of failed dreams:

In the Shreve High football stadium,
I think of Polacks nursing long beers in Tiltonsville,
And gray faces of Negroes in the blast furnace at
Benwood,
And the ruptured night watchman of Wheeling
Steel,
Dreaming of heroes.
'Autumn Begins in Martins Ferry, Ohio'

After school Wright spent two years in the army, including time in Japan, and then on the G. I. Bill studied at Kenyon College, Ohio, where John Crowe Ransom taught. He learned from Ransom 'the Horatian ideal': a poem with 'a single unifying effect'. In 1952 he married and with a Fulbright Scholarship attended the University of Vienna, where he studied German literature. During this time he decided to teach. Again without knowing the faculty, he matriculated at the University of Washington.

Possessed of a photographic memory, which enabled him to recite enormous amounts of poetry, Wright went on to teach at the University of Minnesota for six years before being denied tenure because of heavy drinking and missing classes, followed by two years at Macalester College in Saint Paul and then at Hunter College in New York, where he taught courses on the eighteenth-century novel, Dickens (the subject of his doctoral dissertation) and Hardy. His reputation well-established by his poems and translations, he and his wife began to spend time in Europe, particularly favouring Italy. He died in 1980 of throat cancer.

Hugo's Italy, unlike Wright's, evoked memories of war service. He published a book of poems, *Good Luck in Cracked Italian* (1969): 'I only came / to see you living and the fountains run'. Though he also wrote a collection on the island of Skye, Hugo is best remembered as a poet of the northwest. He said of his inspiration: 'I often found the sources of poems in the lonely reaches of the world, the ignored, forlorn, and, to me, beautiful districts of cities, like the West Marginal Way area in Seattle, the sad small towns of Washington and Montana, the villages and countryside of Southern Italy, wherever I imagined life being lived as amateurishly as we had once played basketball.' He wrote of his use of the West Marginal Way as a place he could 'melodramatically extend and exploit certain feelings' he had about himself tied to his sense of defeat.

What he repeatedly imagined were the landscape's living things, the lonely and the derelict. He returned regularly to the bars of faded towns, in poems like 'The Milltown Union Bar' and 'Death of the Kapowsin Tavern':

Nothing dies as slowly as a scene.
The dusty jukebox cracking through
the cackle of a beered-up crone –
wagered wine – sudden need to dance –
these remain in the black debris.

Although I know in time the lake will send
wind black enough to blow it all away.

Hugo proved consistently critical of his early self ('For many years whenever I did something I was ashamed of, I felt, in addition to the shame itself, a sense of failure'). It is little wonder that he turned at length to psychoanalysis. In *Local Assays: On Contemporary American Poetry* (1985) Dave Smith, who knew him, noted that 'His poems depend upon his own hard self-accusations: he drinks too much, he wastes himself, he lacks courage, he is fat, ugly, uneducated, unsophisticated, inferior, an orphan'. Hugo knew he could work with this. In *The Triggering Town: Lectures and Essays on Poetry and Writing* (1979) he wrote, '*How you feel about yourself* is probably the most important feeling you have'. He knew, he wrote, that 'An act of imagination is an act of self-acceptance', even in the very act of rejection.

In *31 Letters and 13 Dreams* (1977) he published an autobiographical collection, inevitably a talky one. He had been struggling and made no bones about it. His problems with drinking and memories are foregrounded:

On good days, this
is just a town and I am just a lonely man, no worse
than the others in the bar, watching their lives thin
down
to moments they remember in the mirror and those
half
dozen friends you make in life
'Letter to Libbey from St. Regis'

What Thou Lovest Well Remains American (1975) is more robust, despite exploiting Hugo's past humiliations ('I think of Dumar sadly because a dancehall burned / and in it burned a hundred early degradations') and depressions ('hours alone in bars with honest mirrors'). It also offers portraits of other casualties and atmospheric description:

That goose died in opaque dream.
I was trolling in fog when the blurred
hunter stood to aim. The chill gray
that blurred him amplified the shot
and the bird scream.
'Again, Kapowsin'

In the title poem of *White Center* (1980) Hugo comes home. He had hitherto avoided this because, 'With the strange town... you owe the details nothing emotionally', while his home town, 'seemed blocked by allegiances to memory'. Yet the title poem ends on an optimistic note: on the absence of a feeling of shame. *The Right Madness on Skye* (1980) seemed a gamble, though was partly redeemed by his sense that the landscape twinned with his own ('The sky, water, vegetation and wind are Seattle. / The panoramic bare landscape's Montana').

In the late poems, the vein seems a little thinner, but Hugo rallies with his Wright poem, with 'Confederate Graves in Little Rock' and 'Making Certain It Goes On'. Finally, in the title poem, he rises again to optimism, a mood he believed always marked his approach, whatever the critics wrote. Here we are at the Big Blackfoot River, where the speaker and his wife imagine a rejuvenated landscape and a thriving community.

Hugo always felt a debt to James Wright, who had been an early champion of his poetry. There are a number of references to it in Wright's selected letters, *A Wild Perfection* (2005). In July 1958, he wrote to Robert Bly (then editor of *The Fifties* and later a close friend and collaborator on translations) that he thought Hugo's poems shared with Gary Snyder's 'the new imagination' and that he had submitted his friend's manuscript to the University of Minnesota Press from motives of friendship, admiration and guilt 'that a tremendous poet, who is doing something to catch his time and place *alive*' is being ignored. Later he took the manuscript to show Bly.

In a similarly self-deprecating mood Wright wrote in March 1959 to James Dickey, who was still making a name for himself, noting the parallels between Hugo and Dickey (they were the same age, both war veterans and both worked outside academia). He also stressed Hugo's admiration for Dickey's work, always an incentive to the fiercely competitive Dickey. The two corresponded, which greatly pleased Wright. He was not as successful in impressing Donald Hall (then editor of *The Paris Review*) with his friend's poems.

In another letter Wright mentioned that his 'On Minding One's Own Business' came out of a fishing expedition with Hugo on Lake Kapowsin. Hugo reciprocated in remembering their trips in his 1977 'Letter to Wright from Gooseprairie'. And in a late poem, 'Lament: Fishing with Richard Hugo', Wright returned again to the old days and the private joke about a tavern owner they disliked.

The two poets occasionally exchanged visits, though Wright could be an intolerable guest, as he was in early 1959 when he spent days drinking and playing the same Delius record for hours at a time. He had been obsessed by deadlines, with his wife's recent breakdown and a female student he longed to see. In defence of his friend, Hugo later wrote that with Wright's leaving 'some winning energy, tiresome yet important, had just left our life'.

Aside from *A Run of Jacks*, Wright's most public praise came twelve years later in a piece for *The American Poetry Review* entitled 'Hugo: Secrets of the Inner Landscape'. Writing in an idiosyncratic mood, he celebrates their fishing trips and the poet's talent: 'I believe that Richard Hugo has become one of the best poets alive, in any language I know'. Hugo acknowledged being 'touched and grateful' for the 'glowing' piece from Wright. He hoped it had not been promoted by guilt at his behaviour during the visit in Missoula.

Wright's own poems are generally easy to admire but not always easy to identify with. In 'A Kind of Overview in Appreciation' Miller Williams argued that they 'are more often than not words out of his own darkness telling us about violence, loss, and death'. It is not so obvious in the formal, early poems of *The Green Wall* (1957) where we feel we might lose our bearings: 'Errina to Sapho', 'Eleutheria', 'Elegy in a Firelit Room' ('The window showed a willow in the west, / But windy dry. No folly weeping there'). What holds us are the twentieth-century moments: 'A Poem about George Doty in the Death House' and the sly 'A Gesture by a Lady with an Assumed Name':

> Lovers she left to clutter up the town
> Mourned in the chilly morgue and went away,
> All but the husbands sneaking up and down
> The stairs of that apartment house all day.

In *Saint Judas* (1959) Wright is more demanding, his seriousness more apparent. Here he takes on the lot of the lost and the damned ('A Note Left in Jimmy Leonard's Shack'). We are to share their pain with the poet since it is, arguably, everyman's. Doty reappears in 'At the Executed Murderer's Grave' ('Wrinkles of winter ditch the rotted face / Of Doty, killer, imbecile, and thief: / Dirt of my flesh, defeated, underground'). In the title poem we meet a Samaritan Judas, 'flayed without hope'.

The Branch Will Not Break and *Shall We Gather at the River* (1968) are famous for their epiphanies and blessings, their simple delights and surrealistic touches. Yet the poet also turns candidly to his own depressions in 'Stages on a Journey Westward', 'Inscription for the Tank', and the indelible 'Outside Fargo, North Dakota':

> Along the sprawled body of the derailed
> Great Northern freight car,
> I strike a match slowly and lift it slowly.
> No wind.

What has been described as another turn in Wright's work came with *Two Citizens* (1973). He could by now, after half a dozen 'crack-ups', write convincingly, 'I have crawled along the edges of plenty / Of scars' ('Son of Judas'). This collection, which Wright claimed he would never reprint, tested his faith in America, as he saw it from abroad. It is a loose collection, a talky one, which only sometimes works ('Ars Poetica: Some Recent Criticism' and 'The Old WPA Swimming Pool in Martins Ferry, Ohio').

His last books, *To a Blossoming Pear Tree* (1977) and the posthumous *The Journey* (1982) are largely concerned with Europe, though when he returns home in memory he finds consolation and community, 'beauty' even, in the hard lives of his working people ('Blood in my body drags me / Down with my brother'). There are still the flashes of grit that fired his earlier work. Among prose pieces, he attains a kind of acceptance in the meditative poem 'The Journey', and in the fine 'The Vestal in the Forum', which ends with identification:

> A dissolving
> Stone, she seems to change from stone to something
> Frail, to someone I can know, someone
> I can almost name.

If Hugo could not repay Wright for his decisive early support, he would always recognise their time together and the talent. The late poem to Wright's memory, 'Last Words to James Wright' has the lines: 'You wanted words to sing the suffering on / and every time you asked the words came willing'. His prose celebration appeared in the posthumous *The Real West Marginal Way: A Poet's Autobiography* (1986): 'No one carried his life more vividly inside him, or simultaneously in plain and in eloquent ways used the pain of his life to better advantage. What maims others often beyond repair maimed him too, but in some miraculous way it also nourished his great talent. It was miraculous too that his obsessive repetitive mind never limited his artistry.'

While they may not have influenced each other's work directly, they shared a great deal beyond their preoccupations and a blue collar perspective: a love for nature, for instance, and a sense of humour. One hears in their comments a similarity of views about the nature of writing and teaching. They were wedded to honesty, plain speaking and occasional sentimentality. They also shared a disarming readiness to confess weakness in their behaviour and error in their pronouncements.

Their differences were clear, too. Hugo found his style early and kept to it (his 'drumming iambics or his stark and alliterative sentences', in Dave Smith's phrase). Wright experimented with formal and free verse, with conventional and deep imagery. For Hugo the wreckage of places is as eloquent of human failure as the portrait of the individuals that Wright is more prone to seek out.

In the 1970s the two exchanged occasional letters. They last met at a White House reception honouring poets in January 1980, where Hugo is said to have been in tears after meeting his gravely ill friend. Wright would die of throat cancer that March at the age of fifty-two; Hugo two years later, at fifty-eight.

Hugo ends his James Wright essay with an account of being in the Greyhound Bus Station in Wheeling, West Virginia in 1963. It was a depressing place, he recalls, and he knew that Martins Ferry lay unseen across the river. He might have been speaking for himself as well as for Wright when he concluded, 'I let that bus station say a lot about where Jim came from and why it was necessary for him to leave, to get away. And why he did get away. And why he didn't.'

Three Poems

CHRISTIAN WIMAN

Dialects and Dithyrambs

The gunned man gathers his groceries,
howdy-do's a local grandma,
and scuffs to his truck.

The radio reminds him to rage.
Liver-y liberals! Like a jar of white worms,
the seethe and glop and blind imbroglio.

What the catfish relish.
Grubs, more like, reticulate as thumbs.
'Member that mammoth spelunkable mouth outta'
Caddo?'

My lexicon surprises you, madam,
as if meat could read?
Stirruped words, yeehawing the zeitgeist.

Left on Murray right on Stone,
left right left right straight on
to the unlubricious sleep.

Who cares? Congress congressing,
Supremes with them thaumaturgical robes, crap-pants
for president, the burp and glop of a rumdumb country.

Meh, dialects and dithyrambs,
houses from the house factory,
words from the word factory,

nightminds squealing being like a slicked piglet.
He manned one once, eight years old at the Roscoe rodeo.
Like to kicked his titties off.

He giggles, the gunned man, hauls his hoard,
sweetie-pies a not-so-pliable wife,
pops a Bud.

How much do you like, he asks.
Meaning dinner.
Meaning lack.

Jamesian

Porcelain, longing, and the science of small regard
estrange him even from his old companion, loneliness.
Her eyes are black as stars that aren't, some vast
pastness implied, and a present made of void.
Antique the sitting room, antique their talk,
but wholly now the notion that has taken hold.
She creams his tea, breaks a cracker in eternity.
Crewel, cruet, butter bell, rose-chintz, ivory.
Outside, outsiders: an engine's insolence,
laughter, hammer, something coming down.
There are times, prevarications of the air,
a room a realm, civilities, declivities,
even the steam's in code. Laughter. Hammer.

Reading Steinbeck

– and the sorrows hardened,
and in the first light grew palpable, pliable,
and the man fashioned from his a kind of cutter,
and the woman made a rake,
and down the rows, which were the rows of time,
they moved, soiled, famished, ripped to instants,
but lifted, too, the man and the woman,
by the climbing sun, and by the breeze of heat,
and by the hard land whose fluency, for now, for no one
save those whom life had scathed to faith,
they were –

Eight Poems

MARA-DARIA COJOCARU

Translated from the German by Jamie Osborn

Apropos Mr Goselmanu

So, I'm his cat, renowned
Right back to the Egyptians
For bringing blood
Pressure down, and
Once the old man saw
How things stood for his soul's rest
He first of all
Withdrew from sleep
Then the crafty bastard
Plunged me into the river, deep
In a bottle of
Sugarglass and
Hallucinogens. I diligently licked
Substance – the effect
Was: Darwin
Bit my claws off
Indeed
Mr Goselmanu's blood pressure sank and
Meanwhile I drank, found
Myself, as the bottle-walls
Dissolved
In his gentle hand – ever since
I'll purr when plucked
From the water

Dearest,

Dearest hero shrew, I'd love to be so
Strong as you. After each catastrophe
Not only does my spine ache
Continually, I remain always always
I, too... would love to have a heart like you
To leap into the punctuated.

Equilibrium

Mornings, first thing: watering the horses

Of most things, we do not know
Why we – perhaps

Among the philosophical foals
On the meadow in the snow

The way these things
The animals, the ground

The air, one's own scent
Lose, in nostrils

Themselves, form, idea
When we visit the mothers

To be and, early in the morning, go
As shadows to water the horses

A kind of bugging operation, the sun eclipses itself

I still cast a shadow, half, alone, total
Silence, apparently. The blackbird chatters on. The

Whinnying of one horse, stamping of another. The raven
Croaking. Corvids being songbirds. It wasn't

A raven at all. It was a businessman. Or his child
It is the most delicate suit-wearers who so heavily

Enthuse. Everything rings true and the flood bursts
But the goldfinch is sitting and chirping right next to me

And the starling. And the dipper. And the dove
Cooing, what else. And the long-tailed tit

Dictating to the blue. And the pet pricking his
Floppy ears. And any well-bred human

Knows to rejoice at this: this nature. The picnicking couple
Listen in, nodding fervently, silently. Yes; and yet the sun

Has eclipsed itself: click, you missed it

Fish oil: marred

I feel like it helps
Naturally the feeling helps: fish oil
For post-traumatic stress

I the feeling, I have to tell it to this little
Fish, little fish, dead
Fish, deep water, red snapper
Deeper, smeary horizon

But the women do not say
Stop – the crude oil drilling
They say: drill baby. Deep drilling
Uncertainty, slippery doubt, what will a
Snapper not nibble away. He misses
His larvae, but that's nothing
Compared to the bluefin tuna: assault
On the heart's cells. No, really, this is
The intention-to-treat principle
Come, my love, psychoeducation. I feel
Like it only helps women
I am touched. *My love story came to an end*
Drill, baby, drill. I don't know
Whether it helps me: but I'll say it once again
Therapy-disaster dispersant
*There was absolutely nothing**

No fish swims in the nursery
No fish oil dulls the pain
No fish can *explain the depression*
That we see. No oil, no fish

*Said the deep sea diver on the radio, who didn't know what she ought to say, and

To those who follow in our wake: instead of subjugation

The other day, the Lemures came back
Critical, simply threatened with extinction
*What is wrong with you**

I didn't mean it
I cannot understand it
I speak only for myself

I put my ears back
I shroud my tusk
I roll onto my back

I show off my throat
I acidise my shell
I stay stock still

I spread myself flatter on the ground
I assume your favourite colour
I smack my lips as I do

I laugh
I take myself from the field
I take myself off for preening

I scratch you however you like
I give what I'd stored away
I sit back down

I tickle your pelt
I bash my head straight through the brick wall
I rub up against you

I swim in sync with you
I speak from now forever softly
I jerk you off

I remove myself *ad libitum*
I bestow on you my tailfeathers
I snarl at you

I stick your finger in my eye
I adorn your house for you
I seek to be near you

I help you with your offspring
I curtail my own
I kiss my partner

And: I am sorry without end

*And what is *Halbnaturen* supposed to mean

What to do in an emergency: encounter with problem cow

Keep calm. The cow is used to people
If the cow is on the run, show her the way
If the cow is drunk, sing her to sleep
(A tip: cows like Leonard Cohen)

Record the problem. You can't see a problem
Where did it happen? What happened? No
Answer, back to where it all began
Waiting for questions! That's where we have a problem

Make safe. Weigh the problem and
Book extra baggage. Look out
For threatened calves. Take marked escape routes
(Dial YVONNE/986663). You are on your way
To work, but your employer only allows
Dogs? Teach the cow to sit. You'll
See soon enough. Don't take the lift

VI.

(From Capital Ring) [Latitude: 51.5770, Longitude: -0.1416 – Latitude: 51.5769, Longitude: -0.1413; Date: April, May]

Once again eternal spring. Californian blueblossom. Atlantic
Bluebells. The way joy in it fades with the fruiting and always
Smouldering sweetness. The mosquitoes, too early, and squirrels hoarding
Week after week, like our neighbour, for the apocalypse
I play god with the spider and her prey. *The plight of the bumblebee*
Humming behind me. I spin my thoughts, I lose the thread
Sympathise: the bumblebee, the spider, snagged, I'm the dumbest
Not in my backyard. I've interfered. That is Nature

Then the thought turns sticky
All day long won't let me go
Become a flight controller, cosmic
Referee. Heaven forbid

Mara-Daria Cojocaru

in conversation with

JAMIE OSBORN

Mara-Daria Cojocaru is a German poet and philosopher, resident in London. Among the awards she has won across her four books of poetry, Anstelle einer Unterwerfung *(Instead of Subjugation, 2016) and* Buch der Bestimmungen *(Field Notes, 2021), are the German Prize for Nature Writing, the Poetry Prize of the Mondseeland and the Alfred Gruber Prize.*

The following conversation was conducted via email between May and June 2022.

Jamie Osborn: Your poems deal with extinction, animal cruelty, the lack of understanding between species. But I think what first sparked my interest was your sense of humour. The opening poem in your book Anstelle einer Unterwerfung, *'An die Nachgeborenen', takes its title from a Brecht poem and has something of his earnestness. Yet there's a playfulness in the way you treat the catalogue of the poem and the tolerating of anthropomorphism. It's a dynamic I see again in the archness of that immortal cat in 'Apropos Herr Goselmanu', I think?*

MDC: I am always greatly relieved when people find humour in my poems. You are right that most of my poetry takes its starting point in the confrontation with pretty drastic, sad or stupefying aspects of human–animal relations but I have never written a poem on, say, factory farming *simpliciter*. Poetry allows us to eschew simple propositions, for ambiguity and surprise. And I think the same is true of humour, isn't it? At least if it is not of the thigh-slapping kind. In German, we have a word for a particular kind of humour: 'hintersinnig', which is usually translated as 'with a deeper meaning' but I am not sure depth is what makes this word work for me when I think about humour. Instead, humour can help us reach *behind* the obvious, without obfuscating things or being self-important. Often when people talk and think about things such as extinction or our limited understanding of other species, the tone can get a little solemn, misanthropic and desperate. If I feel that way, that honestly kills every poetic impetus I might have, which is why humour works as a good antidote. I don't mean to make light of such feelings and concerns. They can be legitimate. But I can't see that wallowing in them allows for poetry I would want to read myself. For the really depressing things, I read the news. In my opinion, poetry shouldn't be an echo chamber for what we all know is true, but a way to access another layer of meaning that lies behind what is obvious. Again, that meaning needn't be deeper, but it can just broaden my horizon, make me curious and maybe more forgiving.

'Forgiving' is interesting here. It's a term I don't often come across in criticism or reflections on poetry (maybe that's just what I read). What do you think is behind your hesitation in saying that?

The hesitation almost certainly came through the process of writing, since I wrote everything just as it came into my mind, first draft, close to how I would speak. I probably felt that 'curiosity' by itself is not necessarily what I value, but I do when it is inflected by a moral attitude. With understanding, I think that forgiveness can come, so maybe that is the emotional coloratura that I am looking for. I distrust simple activism and I find poems that are simply activist rather abhorrent: 'Look – how awful – here is a metaphor to amplify the sense of despair – oh, dear – how pretty – let us do something – or else!' Poems can make us smarter than that by irritating habits of thinking and feeling while, at the same time, offering us some kind of reassurance that we can promote goodness and beauty (if that doesn't sound too pompous), that maybe there is a place for us ridiculously hyperpowered, world-devouring but loving creatures after all. Maybe!

'Irritating habits of thinking and feeling' – I like that! Looping back, is there also a kind of self-deprecating humour in your approach to science? We're taught (at least, I was) that science is either all reduction or daring and exploration. The semi-ominous, semi-ridiculous figure of Herr Goselmanu stalks through your poems (I think he's a researcher?) and he seems to both provide a foil for the strangeness of looking at nature in the same way that binomials or charts or figures do. Am I misreading that?

Oh, yes, good old Charles Goselmanu. He definitely is a comical figure and one that allows me to undermine the hubris that is built into the various systems of omnipotence he represents. In a way, he is a bit of a poetic father figure, but one that is poetic despite itself. He is science-cum-religious-fervour incarnate, and, in some sense, the poems want to please him but, of course, they can't. A man like Goselmanu doesn't have time for poetry and all subtle humour is lost on him. I should add that I have deep respect for the scientific method – to the extent that I understand it. I meant to study zoology but never did. I am sure that many of the scientific breakthroughs would not have been possible if researchers didn't take themselves and their careers pretty seriously. And still, there is something ever so slightly absurd in this quest for knowledge. That is especially pronounced in the context of animal experimentation, which is something that Goselmanu would have done, too. Doesn't it beggar belief that we humans – after all, socially organised primates with one of the closest mother-child-bonds in the animal kingdom – needed scientists to repeatedly torture rhesus monkeys to find out that touch is vital for an infant? I don't write about that experiment in particular, but Goselmanu is the kind of man who could, very earnestly, be motivated to uncover a fundamental truth about mankind – one that, actually, his own mother could have told him.

I think one of the things I find intriguing (and difficult to translate) in your poems, is a tension between the quest for knowledge that Goselmanu represents and the 'hintersinnig' (which for me has echoes in English in 'hinterland'). In translation that difficulty manifests in the choice between denotative and – not connotative I think, but maybe more structural meanings. To come at it from another angle, I'm interested in your use of form. Both Anstelle *and* Bestimmungen *are organised around chapters or sections of poems in blocks of particular forms. I read this as a kind of experiment, as well as an ordering. Yet the forms begin to unravel as the poems progress – which was a particular challenge in translating them! What's the rationale behind your use of form?*

It definitely has more to do with experimenting than with ordering. I have sometimes heard that, if you read poems of mine that differ in form, you wouldn't necessarily think that they are by the same author. And I am glad that this is so. Sometimes, you get writers who become very comfortable with one particular form and then that is that. They put whatever material interests them through that form like a butcher puts meat, salt and whatever through a mincer and voilà – out comes a popular poem. I can't do that. It may sound a little odd but the reason I end up writing poetry is typically not that I want to publish poems. It's more that poetry allows me to use language in a way that suits my purpose and that purpose changes over the course of time and given different contexts. So, for instance, in *Anstelle einer Unterwerfung*, there is one cycle that deliberately takes anthropomorphism too far, in each poem, and it sort of balances that with a fairly strict form that leaves no doubt of how artificial everything is that goes on in the poems. By contrast, poems that want to bear witness and let the events and creatures speak for themselves, like the ones that feature in a different chapter, are more loose, almost like hasty protocols of the poetic experience of bearing witness in that way. Similarly, in *Buch der Bestimmungen*, I experiment with field notes and geographic coordinates in various ways. In each case, there is a different 'Grundstimmung', if you will, that requires a change of form and could not be successfully captured within or translated into other forms. Whether these experiments with form can be satisfactorily translated into different languages, I don't know. I always felt your translations to be extremely congenial, but I am not a native speaker. Maybe the poems require different forms in other languages and I am open to suggestions.

The one thing that does, I think, stay the same and should stay the same, even in other languages, I feel, is the tone, the emphasis on musicality, the touches of humour. We talked about that.

I notice that while you play with language and enjoy puns, made-up words and slips in the fabric of sound, you maintain the traditional German capitalisation of nouns and capitals at the start of new lines. While many contemporary German poets do away with capitalisation altogether, you seem to use it both as a marker of distinction and as a way of creating ambiguity (I'm often unsure whether a word at the start of one of your lines is a capitalised noun or a verb). This might seem like quite a limited question but it speaks to me about the deceptiveness of some of your poems, like one of those optical illusion cards that I had as a kid: when you move your head, the image shimmers and changes. I suppose I'm asking this partly because I'm not sure I've managed successfully to translate that effect!

I like the idea of poems like optical illusion cards! Yet my use of capitalisation has more to do with production than with effect. I still want the author to be deliberate about the ambiguities they bring about in their poetry. That sounds terribly conventional, but I feel I want to know whether something is meant to be ambiguous or whether the author just couldn't care less about capitalisation and just happily accepts that doing away with it adds another potential meaning. I remember with my first book of poetry, my editor actually did ask me why I didn't write everything small... because that would be the 'modern thing to do'. That seemed so pointless to me that I probably had to rebel against that. Another element to explain the use of capital letters is the importance of line breaks in my poetry. I am quite a fan of enjambments and I feel that the emphasis I place on them is highlighted through starting a new line with a capital letter.

Finally, I want to come to politics: you teach moral and political philosophy, and are interested in the ways in which philosophy and politics are applied. It seems to me that the poems you wrote during the pandemic, which are included in Buch der Bestimmungen *display a more specific and time-bound focus on political circumstance than some of your earlier work, which has a more general approach to animal consciousness. I'll admit part of the reason I touch on this is that I get annoyed at the often-repeated statement that all writing is political – because if everything is political then it defeats the object of definition, doesn't it?*

I think there is more than one question here. First, how do I relate to the statement that all writing is political? I think that is very likely nonsense. Not only is my shopping list not political in the most basic sense in which 'political' is usually defined, namely that which concerns all members of a particular political entity. It also seems that not writing about something would then also be political because you can read so much into any kind of omission. For instance, does the fact that I did not sign a particular petition allow for the interpretation that I am unpolitical on the matter? I don't think so. I appreciate that, in an age of online activism and virtue signalling, people can be very quick to arrive at such judgments but I think that is wrong. It's a bit like with letting go of capitalisation tout court. I want to retain some sense of authorship and agency over the commitments I make, and though I appreciate that politics is more than voting in elections, I find it overbearing and unfruitful to politicise everything.

The second question is whether the poems I wrote during the pandemic are more political. I don't think so. Perhaps I was privately more affected by politics, but I am not sure that is what it means to be political. If we look at the final chapter of Buch der Bestimmungen: it is a cycle of fifteen poems that I co-authored with one of our dogs, meaning that I took the notes for the poem during walks with him and wrote it in hexameter to account for the six feet – four canine, two human – that were walking together. We started that project in December 2019 and, at the time, I was still awaiting the decision on my application for pre-settled status in the UK. So, there was a heightened sense of being a foreigner in this country that I sort of refracted through the lens of being, in virtue of being human, a foreigner in nature. The pandemic certainly brought that to the fore, too. The fragility of human life on earth given the almost biblical curse of losing our breath, our sense of smell, our abilities to commune with our families and neighbours and so on. It sort of further alienated humans from the rest of nature and from human nature or brought that alienation into sharp relief. It is no accident that many people turned to other animals and the environment in search for solace. But, at least thus far, with little insight or lasting effect. If there is a political agenda in that poetry cycle, then it has more to do with trying to stay with that sense of alienation and not seeking refuge in the old anthropocentric ways of thinking and feeling.

Days of Sail

GREGORY O'BRIEN

for Robin White, sea-rider, HMNZS Otago, Torpedo Bay – Raoul Island – Nuku-alofa May 2011,
and for the Fifita family, the dancers and the tapa-makers

The common thread, eye of a whalebone
needle, this lifelong stitching together of

that which belongs: sailcloth, canvas,
the air when last you

breathed it. Robin, I remember long hours on deck
  and how
the ratings, when they couldn't explain a naval
  protocol

or phrase, would simply shrug and tell us, 'It must
  have been
passed down from the Days of Sail...'
  as each day is itself, in turn, passed down

or arrives unannounced: the sea when last we sailed it –
folds, creases and seams of the Great Tapa.
  I take home what I can

the poem a pin-hole camera, a letting in
of what little light is allowed it. I remember

you walking the breadth of Raoul Island barefoot –
the three-hour Denham Bay round-trip –

to absorb the animal warmth and sentience
of that steaming, vented volcano.

Later we noted as many stars in the ocean
as in the night sky – those same

luminous bodies rising to the surface
like feeding fish. Such were the nights

and days of sail and barkcloth, whale-song and
footfall on remote islands –

the voyage ending, as a voyage must
with dancing: on the Nuku-alofa harbourfront

flickering costumes of the lakalaka reflected
in the floor's dark polish. I think of you and Michael

and the fabric in which a life is wrapped – the acres and
nautical miles of pummelled bark

and sailcloth, a sleeping mat on Kiribati,
a tent flapping at Victory Beach and

the reappearance of your wedding dress at
Otakou Marae after fifty years. Such things the tapa
  notices

and records: common threads, each voyage
as it ends, and the dancing that will never stop – these

inexhaustible days of sail
    as handed down to us – bright fabrics, swirling.

Jon Glover

In conversation with

RORY WATERMAN

RW: You became involved in several publications during your student days at Leeds University in the 1960s: the student magazine Sixty-One, Poetry *and* Audience *and, of course,* Stand. *Was this a particularly exciting time for a young poet, and Leeds a particularly exciting place to be one?*

JG: On reflection, it was exciting. Though I want to say immediately that I was not self-consciously 'a young poet', and excitements about whom I met – student journal organisers and editors, student poets, published poets (staff, visitors, Fellows), when and where I met them, how and why I met them – were factors intimately and 'locally' linked to the daily human contacts and feelings of 'studentdom'. So, on reflection, from the second year of my BA English Literature and Philosophy (1963–4), the sense of a writing buzz came from meetings, especially in the Mouatt-Jones Coffee Lounge and the Student Union bar. From our present times of popular, practice-led, and writer-orientated BA to PhD programmes in the 2020s, it is strange to look back at 'student-led' programmes (for that is what they were) working at sophisticated and self-consciously standard-led, policy-led and creativity-led opportunities being there sitting next to a fascinating person over coffee.

Of course, there are tales to tell about who our lecturers were – poets and editors with first-hand contacts with writers and writing in the publishing worlds. So, a question I ask now is: was the student-led excitement and infectiveness a natural spin-off from the curricula and lecturers with whom we met and talked incessantly? And the question after that is how and where did the Leeds 'student-led' writing and publishing drive come from? I was going to write 'publishing atmosphere' but that doesn't 'get' the actual force and need.

What tales? What interactions did you have with, say, Geoffrey Hill? What effects did these interactions have on you at the time?

I arrived in Leeds from grammar school Surrey in October 1962, aged nineteen. My first interaction with Hill was in a first-year lecture; he gave several to new students, mainly on poets and poetry. Other lecturers, taking their turns, included Arnold Kettle, member of the Communist Party, giving a socialist view of novels, and Head of Department Norman Jeffares, who spoke on Yeats and his personal meeting with Maud Gonne. In the 2010s I found, in my attic, my hand-written notes derived from Hill's lectures, inter alia on Owen and Rosenberg, vaguely written and poorly 'recorded'. At the same time, I found Hill's own text for the lectures I had heard, archived in Leeds University's Special Collections. A strange and humbling 'interaction'. We students had heard subtle and personal insights from one of the great English poets. By the end of the 1964–5 academic year, I had had interactions with poet, editor and critic Jon Silkin, with poet and ex-London Group member Peter Redgrove, with poets Ken Smith, Bill Price-Turner, Jeffrey Wainwright and others, through living in Silkin's flat with Elaine Shaver, my wife to be, while Silkin was away taking part in the Edinburgh Festival.

'Our present times of popular, practice-led, and writer-orientated programmes.' What did you make of the proliferation of creative writing courses in the latter stages of your subsequent university teaching career? What has been lost and what, if anything, gained, since the milieu you describe as a student at Leeds?

Until the 1970s no UK Universities offered degrees in creative writing. Perhaps this is odd since much of the planning of degree 'content' in the UK was heavily influenced by what UK academics saw as intellectually worthy in the USA, where creative writing had long been part of BA and more advanced awards if not leading to named creative writing degrees. I saw and was part of much of the change. For example, as a *Poetry & Audience* and *Sixty-One* editor I was constantly aware of the challenges to understand, justify and change (why, how, what) through discussion. I was conscious of writing as 'doing', as 'performing' for myself and for others, and of the personal soul-searching and soul-changing in deciding to accept poet X's poem for publication whilst recognising its challenges or confirmations to one's own work. Editing with others on a weekly basis, and fitting, or not fitting, with Redgrove's weekly workshops, and the performances of guest poets, meant change, embarrassment, anger with friends and shock with loved ones.

The years 1965–6 saw me in charge of the Leeds Students' Arts Festival. On principle it was for people in all of the Leeds Universities and Colleges and the public, and it was intended for the students to learn from and be entertained by. Their creative work stood with that of the professionals. Not for assessment marks but for success and impact as Art. I organised, with help and advice from Jon Silkin, a Conference on Literature of War. Speakers included Silkin himself, Michael Hamburger and Dennis Welland, international expert on Wilfred Owen. Again, not for marks but for interest. Poets reading included Hill, Redgrove, Silkin, Ken Smith and Bill Price-Turner – not on prescription, as it were, but because we wanted to hear and meet them. Between 1965 and 1967 we met and worked with Gregory Fellow David Wright, a wonderful poet, editor and person.

In the summer of 1966 I moved to Elmira, New York so that my wife, Elaine, could complete her BA. Before coming to Leeds for her Junior Year Abroad, she had taken various modules in creative writing. She was used to the concept and practice of creative writing for progressive learning and assessment. In the Elmira College autumn term I was invited to offer a creative writing module for voluntary mature students. I learned a lot in the upstate NY environment and used ('used'!) a lot of the writing techniques and interactions that I had learned.

What changes, for good or ill, did you observe between those burgeoning years of creative writing at British universities and your final years at the University of Bolton?

The present Tory government is effectively attacking the performing arts and practical creative arts education through schools and universities. This is different from writers doubting or even attacking themselves. My experience has confirmed for me that the systematising through 'validation processes', through assessment, with internal and external examiners, through the rewards and implied admiration of Degree Certification, remain very worthwhile, and may well continue to develop in importance, particularly as social media makes 'validation' with and from public interest, and availability, increasingly real. I am impressed by the ways that, for example, university libraries are making 'teaching and learning' responsive to and with the electronic universal availability of what for me and my predecessors was locked in single shelf-bound copies. I like to think that the sciences, social sciences and technologies are very much dependent on, and pleased with, social and personal interconnections, with learning and living together. Poetry and publishing, creating and reading, are social. Will we have to fight the Tories for this creative socialism?

How should we do that?

I have had, still have, very important experiences of working, thinking and discovering with others – as a student myself, with my working-life students, with fellow workers in publishing, with members of the WEA and local writing groups. Even if an individual may in various ways be 'group-conscious', she or he may write in intensively personal, original ways. I like to think that from primary school to post-doctoral lives our organisations and democratic structures will allow and encourage creative meetings. Organised education does not require obedience and routine rules. My perception at present is that the Tory government, including educational policy-making and sponsorship of the arts, is neither familiar with this, nor interested. I see 'creative socialism' as a merger of political socialism and the common (!) shared experiences of writing, reading, discussing. Thus, de-facto opposing Toryism.

I also see this 'socialism' as a way of following the poetics of Geoffrey Hill. In his later poetry and lectures he followed Wittgenstein's approach to language – poetry follows language as words in action, not the sources of hidden meanings 'behind'. As poets in groups – classroom or home or publishers – we can learn from the actions we share.

In 2009, August Kleinzahler told the Guardian *that he thought university creative writing programmes were 'unsavoury': 'It's terrible to lie to young people, and that's what it's about', he said. How would you counter that statement? Presumably you would.*

I am sure that Kleinzahler's ready readers and familiar scholars will have happy glosses on the poet's views on university creative writing programmes. I can imagine why a great, individual and successful American, having worked in various well-spaced-out cities and universities, might worry about, or despise, conventional, assessable, outcome-led programmes. Kleinzahler might think that fee-dependent and student-number-drawn universities might be scared of inspiring dissent and shock, apparently validating graduation by frightening and unemployable Certificated Writers. And he might think that a course unable to scare and disable will automatically not lead to Keats or Eliot or Ginsberg or himself. So close the art schools, the conservatoires, the dance and drama schools.

I like to think that people can choose and select their preferred levels of personal risk, and that group interaction, friendship and support can help to manage (in all senses) risk. Maybe there are serious risks in studying Shakespeare or learning to dance *The Rite of Spring*. Or studying medicine or psychiatry or astrophysics. Does Kleinzahler think that creative writing is the only risky programme? I am sorry for him if he does. I have enjoyed and been thrilled by working with future writers for whom risk was the reason they were there. One of the most wonderful writers I helped through a creative writing PhD and into publishing books and giving reading tours was tetraplegic. Though perhaps he helped me and the others in his group as much as being helped. Owen Lowery-led creative 'socialism' indeed.

Surely the American context is far from democratic, further still from socialist: it seems every poet in the US more or less has to get an MFA as a rite of passage, and those have to be paid for, too. Aren't you therefore at risk of over-romanticising, even if Kleinzahler is rather emphatically missing the point?

I haven't taught, or tried to be published, in the US for many years. Does the average US fresher in Eng-US Lit with creative writing get taught that on graduation they will need to submit a relevant degree certificate with every submission of poem, story or play script to a creative journal or publishing house? My hunch is, from the writers and artists I know, that commitment to writing will be found without a publishers' railway seat or commercial flight ticket, and that writers will, as has often happened in the past, find a friendly, interested publishing house, or will found their own. Or will campaign for new methods, styles and aims in how writing becomes visible. The US, and increasingly the UK, are surely aware of the prestige, energy and possible profit to be made through reflecting the new and unrecognised.

At Leeds, you joined a workshop run by Peter Redgrove. The poet Victoria Field once told me about attending workshops in his Hobsbaum-inspired Falmouth Poetry Group in the 1970s and 80s, and they sounded equal parts rewarding and foreboding.

Redgrove was a Gregory Fellow, paid to be there, to be visible and contactable. And essentially to get on with his own writing and for such writing to be shared. The English Department played no role in publicising his presence. Students in the University found that other students had run, written for, printed, 'published' and SOLD their own magazines. Famously, Leeds had the weekly 1d magazine *Poetry & Audience*, run by undergraduates with a few postgraduates. Gregory Fellows, through Union pigeonholes, contacted editors and submitted their work. They would meet, informally, in the Student Union or the pub. They offered to give readings and the Student English Society and *P&A* organised several readings by past or present Fellows or by other contacts. Unusually, with it not being a requirement, Redgrove offered Hobsbaum-style, weekly creative writing seminars. They were completely voluntary, with no entry-requirements and no assessments, and students brought their own cyclostyled poems for open discussion. Redgrove submitted his own new work. As I remember, other members of the group read out your 'poem for today' and, as in the Hobsbaum method, you listened to the discussion of what you'd written but did not join in or 'introduce' till later. You had to learn what the poem 'did' without your pre-spoken support. Redgrove was pleasant, friendly and supportive.

Jon Silkin has of course been a huge influence on your literary life, and that started with Stand. *How did you meet, and what did you make of him then? In your introduction to Silkin's* Collected, *which you co-edited, you make the point that he, too, was very approachable. He already had some reputation then, and so did* Stand.

The visibility and active presence of poets at the University of Leeds in the 1960s was, by students, taken for granted. Silkin became a Gregory Fellow for two years in 1958. Apart from two years' National Service and evacuation as a schoolboy to Kent, then to Swansea, then to isolated rural Wales, he had lived in or near London, and never previously been to the North. After the end of his Fellowship, he stayed on in his University-rented flat in Headingly, edited *Stand*, carried out research on war poets and continued his own writing. He was very visible in the Student Union and through readings. I probably first saw him while I was studying in the large round British Museum-style Brotherton Library. He was walking through tables to exit doors at the back. I later realised this was to see the Head of Libraries.

Students took it for granted that they would found, write for, edit and sell journals – on film, theatre, politics and poetry. Each journal would have a table and would shout out their titles for custom. I was selling *P&A* and Silkin was selling *Stand* from the next table. Dialogue between sellers and buyers, and between the editorial staff behind the tables, was non-stop. By summer 1965, Elaine and I were regular visitors to Jon's flat in Headingly, which was also the Head Office of *Stand*. Later that summer, Jon, with his partner and his co-editor Ken Smith left for a fortnight at the Edinburgh Festival, and Elaine and I were left in charge of *Stand*. Later, we walked with Jon through Headingly to visit Geoffrey Hill at his house where Jon was to say goodbye since he and *Stand* were moving to Newcastle. On another day we walked with Jon out for the last time from the house on the Otley Road.

Was Tony Harrison much of a presence? He was in almost every copy of Stand *in the 1970s, or so it seems. Silkin obviously championed him from the start*

Many of us were aware of him, but I didn't meet him face to face till he came to the Student Union, I think in 1965, after time in Africa and Europe. It was the start of many interactions in person, through his plays which I was lucky to see at the National Theatre, through hearing readings, and being at meetings through Silkin and *Stand* in Newcastle where Tony was to live.

What were your aims for Stand *when you took it over, and did they differ in any way from what had gone before?*

Those who had been involved over the years were wary after Silkin's death. We decided to advertise and make a new editor the result of public competition. The results were not happy. I decided to step in with the support and interest of many who had been involved over the years.

Your aim was continuation, then? Is there anything you're particularly proud to have achieved as Stand *editor?*

Elaine and I both lived by Silkin's commitment to openness, involvement, friendship and opportunity. I am now proudest to have had an open door for students and staff. They learned how poetry worked through reading, choosing and doing. Following Elaine's death in 2019, and my worsening MS, I am delighted and humbled that *Stand* continues with John Whale and others who had been personal contacts over the decades. I am proud that many students involved their experience as *Stand* workers in their research and later employment in education and publishing.

Do you feel the scene of little magazines is as healthy now as it has always been?

I understand little of the electronic magazine scene. I think that the old guard, including *Stand* and *PNR*, go on well and strangely, although using many electronic links, maintain a paper base. I have recently been looking at my 1960s copies of *Poetry & Audience*. On reflection I think it had many of the virtues of the swift electronic world of today.

I'm grateful for Silkin's Complete Poems, *which you co-edited with Kathryn Jenner – not least because it contains so many previously unpublished poems. Working through his archive, years after his death, and making all those discov-*

eries, must have been a moving experience.

Working through fifty yards of Silkin shelving in Leeds was moving and surprising, yes. But, having become one of his literary executors, and a collaborator in many fields, it was also a continuation of a life together. I had worked with him and with his many friends and colleagues since 1964–5. His emotions and thoughts were normally public and shared. Writing a poem, for him, was often a process that involved 'could you look at this?' It was not private and hidden and secret. His offer, followed by whatever response, was essential to a public, if complex and surprising, personality. Friends and fellow *Stand* workers took it for granted that writing, editing, publishing, selling, talking and responding were parts of a non-stop human and humane life.

In the book's introduction, you discuss his often expansive method of drafting, specifically in relation to some of those previously unpublished poems. 'The new poems become specific entities in their own right', you write, and 'we have tried to select the most interesting and challenging of the entities that have emerged.' What might make your selected version of a poem more 'interesting' than its counterparts, beyond it being 'challenging' (and is that necessarily a virtue)? Could you give an example?

It is hard to think of Silkin wanting to write, or enjoying the writing of, a 'comforting' or 'lulling' poem. Part of the process of friendship was being accustomed to challenging, being challenged and arguing. A poem, making a poem, re-discovering a poem, was to be part of the normality of argument. And part of the normality of emotional exposure. Having been part of this from life in Otley Road, to Queen's Road and other addresses in Newcastle, opening another box or file in Leeds Brotherton Library Special Collections was, month after month, year after year, in many ways for me something to love as well as something to be frightened by. A privilege and a renewal of friendship.

I would love to be able to feel the papers with Jon Silkin's hand-writing or typing on. Sadly, I am now unable to get to Leeds. I would also love to re-feel the decision-making processes. So often it was not part of a simple choice – this word, this section, this argument, was not just a preferred spelling or choice of adjective. It was part of a bodily involvement in meaning and belief and love.

Do you think Silkin would have wanted in print all of the previously unpublished poems that you included? Does that matter, if the work deserves it? Of course, he left the poems to be discovered – he didn't destroy them all like, say, Basil Bunting seems to have done.

An interesting question. Probably, based on my experience of working with him, he would have been glad (not the same as 'happy') to see so much in print. All so much part of his inner, but shared, arguments with words, himself, others.

The *Complete Poems* contains an appendix reproducing poems that changed between first journal publication and later book presentation. And there are examples showing very different versions of the same poems. We couldn't decide on one proper, most probably favoured by Jon Silkin himself, most liked by us. In many ways, including the variants was right through recognizing poems as never finished, never 'done with'.

Silkin clearly wrote almost daily, and then discarded most of what he'd written. In the same introduction, you write about how he'd jot on submissions to Stand, *for example, if they had arrived unaccompanied by SAEs.*

I am trying hard to remember his writing, alive and physical. I do not have a picture of pages being cast aside in the waste basket. Evolution and change happened because of 'meaning' and 'value' and 'dialogue'. In the Special Collections at Leeds there is evidence of how, for example, the poem 'The Coldness' changed and expanded through a dialogue with poet and friend Emanuel Litvinoff. Litvinoff had written poems in the Second World War, was important in writing about Jewishness and was part of the crucial writing-as-sharing process. Jon asked me – non-Jew, non-religious – to edit the Northern House pamphlet of Litvinoff's poems, *Notes for a Survivor* (1972). Northern House was a series of pamphlets started privately in Leeds by Silkin, Ken Smith and Andrew Gurr, the last from the Department of English. Gurr used an antique printing press made available to him by the Department to demonstrate to students type and typesetting. Gurr typeset and hand printed thousands of copies of Silkin's *Flower Poems*, Smith's *Eleven Poems* and Hill's *Preghiere*. His role in setting Northern House pamphlets by hand was taken up by lecturer John Barnard from 1965. Do it yourself, join the writers, help the readers. My Northern House *The Grass's Time* was my first collection.

Let's talk a little about your own poetry. Your most recent collection, Birdsong on Mars *(2020), ends with twenty-six poems for your late wife, Elaine, written in the early days of the pandemic – a moving, forthright record of disparate uncertainties. You refer to them as 'mock-sonnets'. What drew you to the sonnet for this sequence, in any capacity, and why 'mock'?*

When Elaine was dying from cancer in 2019, I couldn't stop thinking about how poetry had brought us together as students in Leeds and how poetry was becoming an unstoppable part of our parting. The tiniest moments of contact and understanding were, in the fullest sense, terrible. I found that picking up a pen was both freeing and leading to more endings. Glimpses, moments, remembered scenes. Fear, meeting the doctors and nurses who awfully knew what was happening, and sitting with Elaine, increasingly, in silence.

I found that short pieces of language were all I could do. Sonnets were both tiny and gigantic, mathematical, infinite and endless. I wanted her for ever, but I decided to limit speech and love to fourteen lines at a time. Experience of the dying moments was formal and informal, timeless and timed. I couldn't, and didn't want to, crawl up the cliff-faces of 'real' sonnets. I wasn't 'in charge'. But

I found happiness in letting a scene or memory happen for about ten lines followed by about four lines of diversion or re-discovery in another world. After Elaine died, the diversions and re-discoveries went on for ever. 'For ever' went on 'for ever'. What I knew from then on was not real in any conventional sense. It was mock reality, mock knowledge, mock poetry. So, for me and for those who read them, my sonnets may have seemed contained in fourteen or sixteen lines with ten syllables in each – but they were 'mock'.

'For ever.' In the preface to that sequence, you write that it 'is continuing'. And is it still continuing to continue?

Since that terrible time the moments of freedom, discovery and dis-resolution have continued. There are days, years later, when three or four mock sonnets happen together in a couple of hours. I need the process, the risks, the repeated re-ended endings. Will they find a publisher? Recently, I was speaking with Michael Schmidt about Wittgenstein's *Notebooks*, with one 'text' following down on the right hand, recto, pages and a completely different 'sequence' on the left, verso. The recto and verso pages have been separately translated and separately published at very different dates. I have thought of making a version with mock sonnets all grouped on the recto pages and explanatory, prose non-sonnet versions/diversions on the versos.

From the Archive

from *PNR* 239, Volume 44 Number 3, 2018

The Cult of the Noble Amateur

[...] What good is a flourishing poetry market, if what we read in poetry books renders us more confused, less appreciative of nuance, less able to engage with ideas, more indignant about the things that annoy us, and more resentful of others who appear to be different from us? The ability to draw a crowd, attract an audience or assemble a mob does not itself render a thing intrinsically good: witness Donald Trump. Like the new president, the new poets are products of a cult of personality, which demands from its heroes only that they be 'honest' and 'accessible', where honesty is defined as the constant expression of what one feels, and accessibility means the complete rejection of complexity, subtlety, eloquence and the aspiration to do anything well. As Kaur's editor has explained: 'The emotional intensity of Rupi's message of self-empowerment and affirmation, combined with her passionate audience really resonated and we could see through sales of her self-published edition that her readers were really responding to her message.' Similarly, Don Paterson, the editor of Tempest and McNish, says McNish appealed to him because of her 'direct connection with an audience' and the 'disarming honesty of the work'.

When did honesty become a requirement – let alone the main requirement – of poetry? Curiously, the obsession doesn't apply to all literature; there is no expectation that the output of novelists or playwrights should reflect their personalities. Yet every one of the reviews and articles relating to McNish in the press in the past two years cites this feature as her work's main selling point. Reviewing her new Picador collection *Plum* in *The Scotsman*, Roger Cox writes:

> It's not that she doesn't care about things like scansion and simile; more that, in her personal list of aesthetic priorities, immediacy and honesty matter more. [...] Much of what McNish has to say urgently needs saying; and if form follows function in her poems, well, that's as it should be.

Honesty as an aesthetic priority? The function of poems? BBC presenter Jim Naughtie delivered similar non sequiturs when interviewing McNish for the BBC News channel's Meet the Author broadcast on 15 June 2017. Asked what audiences like about her poems, McNish answered: 'they like the honesty in them'. [...]

Rebecca Watts

read the full article at www.pnreview.co.uk

This Prison of English

te pāhikahikatanga / incommensurability, Vaughan Rapatahana (Flying Islands) NZ$10
Reviewed by John Gallas

(Please note: this reviewer, though from Aotearoa, is not a Te Reo/Māori speaker/reader. There will be more English, and quotations of Vaughan Rapatahana's English versions of his poems, than there should be).

*

Whatever happened to untamed, un-Agent-filtered, un-English-language-obliged literature? It's here. Little book, great leap-in-the-right-direction.

Splendidly, *te pāhikahikatanga* starts with a quadruple battery against the tyranny of English and plea for a te reo Māori readership: an introductory poem ('Stay alive / I give you a book in Te Reo / Māori / open your eyes / open your ears...'); a quotation by Gary Lachman ('There is no direct substitution of one language for another... different languages express a different way of seeing the world'); an Introduction ('I now write in my first language... because I want to fully express everything in my mind, my heart, in my soul... The English language is crammed full of the subject matter and cultural customs of the lands of Britain...'); and an in-your-face first poem ('Fuck / I can't exist in this language any more / it defeats me... give me an escape from this prison of English').

What follows is 120 pages of Te Reo poems, with accompanying 'versions' in English. 'I have translated these poems into the English language, but not in a "perfect" translation. It's impossible! Thus the title of incommensurability / te pāhikahikatanga'.

Readers who know and have followed Rapatahana's poetry, through, for example, 'ternion', 'ngā whakamatuatanga / interludes', and 'ināianei / now', will recognise much of the contents. There are love poems ('ki te tūāraki', 'he ruri ngāwari', 'he papakupu o aroha', 'kua tekau ngā tau tonu'), poems of mourning for a lost son and broken families ('kāore he mātāmua', 'ko taku whānau', 'te ngākau pōuri o te huaketo'), poems of belonging (Rapatahana lives variously in Aotearoa, Hong Kong SAR and the Philippines – 'āe te henga', 'te taiao Aotearoa', 'ko aotearoa', 'Orongomai', ko taku whare tēnei') and what might be termed nature poems, with their enviromental edge ('ngā wāna', 'ngā rākau', 'he mōtaetea: huringa āhuarangi'). But always amongst them lie the explosions of anger and independence that mark the committance to a language, culture and way of seeing that has been overborne, murdered, ignored, sidelined, snuffed out, embraced-so-as-to-suffocate, and with its history distorted and hushed. We read, we wait, and we get a gentle claim for Māori 'ownership' ('aotearoa... a normal name before an abnormal name / a first people before strangers'). In 'kerikeri' urgency and injustice grow ('ignore the words of this white person / it's time to get real for some white people / real like the original inhabitants of this town'); in 'ko te tāima mō he panoni nui' the consequences of white culture's / language's take-over are laid out ('there are many youths suiciding / too many Māori youths / it is time for new thoughts'); pleas for Te Reo in 'ngā ruri Māori' ('where's our Māori poems / where's our words? / not here / not here') and 'e pīkau ana ahau he riri'; and in 'Rangiaowhia, 1864' ('who knows about the murders at Rangiaowhia? / the terrible deed of the pākehā / the massacre by the white men / we all should know') and 'te pakanga nui o waikato anō?' ('rangiriri, rangiaowhia, ōrākau / who knows about these?') the naked facts of a history tidied away crackle onto the pages.

As it began, the collection ends with a section of 'notes' that contain a fourfold battery on the dominance of English. First, a rational exposition of translating his own poetry into English, reluctant but unavoidable in many ways ('The "solution"? To write in one's indigenous language as much as practicable and to hope, to expect, that readers and listeners aspire to learn it too'); followed by a poem oringally written in English that also 'critiqued this tongue' – 'tongues':

no one around here speaks english.
not because they cannot
but because they don't need to.

This is a many-levelled poem that tackles the issue forthrightly: clearly Rapatahana knows 'other languages' (and other languages than English and Māori) – there is no excuse for us.

The third concluding shot is 'aroha mai, apirana', in which 'Everything I have been saying, then, is summarised in the final poem' –

let's murder this marauder once and for all
ko mate, mate, mate me kāore he ora mō tēnei arero

and finally, the personal struggle, every day, to 'supplicate its fancy frissons / into brute submission' (*it's* being *English's*) and the smiling note

today   i   maybe
won

It is not, however, the wholly admirable fighting of a good fight that makes 'te pāhikahikatanga' such an important and beautiful collection: it is the telling mix of the personal and the public, the different sorrows and contentments, explosions that are not only political but also from daily life, gentleness and humour (even in the combative poems), and the final feeling, to an English reader/speaker, that they are not the rule of thought, expression, feeling, culture and awareness, nor of the expression of these in poetry – that there is a whole world of other people going about their writing and their lives unfiltered by that most awful of literary agents – the English language.

screw the flag of England...
a big bare-arse to this flag
two fingers to this symbol
of injustice...
I want a flag
for all the people
of Aotearoa.

The Mainstream British Lyric

Sarah Wimbush, ***Shelling Peas with My Grandmother in the Gorgiolands*** **(Bloodaxe) £10.99**
Mark Pajak, ***Slide*** **(Cape) £12**
Reviewed by Joey Connolly

It's rare you can trace a poet's influence to a single writer, let alone a single poem, but a number of moments in Sarah Wimbush's debut *Shelling Peas with My Grandmother in the Gorgiolands* seem traceable to a single couplet. The final lines from Carol Ann Duffy's 'Prayer' run:

Darkness outside. Inside, the radio's prayer –
Rockall. Malin. Dogger. Finisterre.

Which isn't a bad choice for a lodestar: it's more or less the jewel in the crown of a very specific poetic tradition. The gravitas-inducing pauses generated by the one-word sentences accumulate toward the release of the heavy rhyme, which works to lift the prosaic and secular (shipping forecast) into the epiphanic and spiritual (the prayer). It's hard to think of a neater exemplar of the mainstream British lyric's whole jam. Compare, from Wimbush's book:

... yearning
for the atchin tans where trees nurse the sun,
the places with whispered names:
Hagg Lane, Mission Springs. The Garden

or, four pages later

... the puff and pout, hands open, slapped.
These men who live by wiser rules.
Outsiders. Set apart. Kings in fact.

or

... above the whiteness he'd excite the air
with tiny circles. I imagined words
like: daughter, sharpen, write.

or, the final lines of the book

... the image of a man digging forever through a coal seam two foot thick. It is black lung and unwritten songs. It is soup kitchens, work vests, hewers. Picks.

But it isn't true that Duffy is the only influence here. 'Our

Jud', a rhyming sonnet anaphorising on 'And' in order to itemise the alternately laudable and reprehensible actions of a male protagonist, is in all of these ways a reprise of Simon Armitage's 'Poem' ('And if it snowed and snow covered the drive...').

Wimbush, then, is straight out of the centre of a mainstream poetic which developed at a time when diversity meant acknowledging poets from 'the regions' – and, indeed, *Shelling Peas...* is heavily invested in singing Yorkshire, and particularly Wimbush's native Doncaster. It does this well, with a canny ear for the vernacular and a characterful, nouny imagery.

Unlike Armitage or Duffy, too, Wimbush can write about the Romany identity which, we assume, she inherits through the titular grandmother. The fact that Romany or traveller experience is (perhaps with the exception of David Morley's work) excluded from the British poetic canon means that these poems bring something of intrinsic worth, even before we come to evaluate their poetic merit. But it's a shame they should have to. Whether there's a risk of reproducing what Sandeep Parmar analyses in her essay 'Not a British Subject' as 'the singular lyric voice [which] should not merely reproduce poetic sameness through an universal "I" or self-fetishizing difference' it isn't really my place to say, but it does perhaps explain why it feels to me that the strongest poems here come when Wimbush pushes through lyric conventions to write something stranger, more disquieting. 'The Calling Basket' detaches from the left margin into centre-alignment, and detaches too from conventions of metaphor-making to leave us asking what's being compared to what:

> Nottingham lace is the pacing green at Thorne horse fair.
> Threads are exotic birds from the Indian subcontinent
> or a front parlour in Rossington. Broderie anglaise
> is filigree cast in a foundry.

By the time this parade of cumulatively unsettling comparison is interrupted by the positively Eliotic 'Centuries on the doors as queens of the Underworld. | Centuries walking the lanes as dust' I'm swept up, sold. This, and several other poems working at this pitch – 'A Sund'y in Worksop', 'Gifts', 'The Powder Monkey's Apprentice', 'Hillards' – elevate *Shelling Peas with My Grandmother in the Gorgiolands* into an interesting collection worthy of attention.

If Wimbush takes Armitage and Duffy as her major influences, Mark Pajak looks (very) slightly aside from the belaurelled canoneers to the former or current editors of major poetry lists Craig Raine and, Pajak's own editor at Cape, Robin Robertson.

In an extravagantly grumpy piece for *The Times*, Graeme Richardson wrote that *Slide*, Pajak's debut, 'has an adolescent fixation on darkness and violence, with imagery that doesn't always ring true'. He's exactly half right, and the fascination with brutality is part of Pajak's inheritance from Robertson. But in terms of the assuredness of its image-making I can think of few debuts of the last decade to rival *Slide*.

Take 'let the fork hold open its little silver palm', or 'footsteps smoke / in the silt'. One blind spot of contemporary British poetry is for non-visual images – but Pajak hears, on a bus, the 'finger-drum of engine pistons'; we feel it as the 'ignition ripples in the black windows'.

The particular strategy of image-making we find in *Slide* is familiar from the 'Martian Poetry' championed by Craig Raine in the eighties. Exhibit A, from Raine: books 'are mechanical birds with many wings'. Compare Pajak, where in reading 'I'd [...] break open a loaf of paper'. Or, exhibit B, Raine: 'Mist is when the sky is tired of flight / and rests its soft machine on ground'. Pajak: 'a chimney hangs from the sky / on a white string'.

But there's a reason this approach to poetry died on its arse forty years ago, and it's that it ensures that even very clever and striking images remain merely images, pretty tokens, Wittgensteinian pictures unable to frame their own context. Their very emphasis on themselves *as* images can't help but imply an aptly Martian indifference towards the human world. Too often here we're left with a clever image which Pajak doesn't seem to be willing to *put to use* in any meaningful sense. A train about to hit a cat might be 'a sentence before the full stop', but it's hard to see what might be made of that. Nor from the underside of a rowboat in 'the shape of a church door':

> how many have opened
> for a man to fall out of a storm
> into that deep quiet.

I don't know, how many *have* opened for a man to fall out of a storm into that deep quiet? Tell us another. If the image sets up a parallel it's between religiosity and death, but nothing in the collection provides any sense as to what this poetry wants us to make of the connection.

It's hard to blame Pajak for following this route. He can't move for prizes and awards. There's an establishment in operation here which – needing to quantify, measure, deliver and hierarchicalise – is more equipped to esteem meaningful-sounding capsules of poem-like text than the chaos of brilliance. Well-defined dramatic situation, honed voice, striking images? First place. Whether it all means anything falls by the wayside.

Where culpability might start to feel appropriate though is when the collection's inability to act on its images seems mirrored on the moral plane. Aestheticising gestures apply equally to horror as to beauty: a starved dog is a 'bin-bag / of cutlery'; a girl's burn scar is 'a small pink socket on her forearm'. The footsteps smoking in the silt is from a portrait of Virginia Woolf drowning herself in the Ouse. Each is described dispassionately, and the vacuum left by authorial directionlessness is filled by an amorality which can feel cold, cruel.

The narrator of 'Crystal' witnesses a girl – she is, the poem discomfitingly observes, 'younger / than eighteen' – being slipped a date-rape drug, and does nothing. His only commentary on his passively facilitating this sexual assault being that 'it's late'; the bar is closing. Even bleaker, two poems later, in 'After Closing Time', we read that:

> Now we are what the world
> considers 'men'. Which is to say

we've learnt that falling is inevitable.

'Falling' in what sense? The 'closing time' link to the date-rape poem insists that we make a connection. We might also reflect on Pajak's depiction of Woolf's suicide as related to a symbolic 'scream': 'Like so many of us it has kettled in her chest / all her life'. This generalising of her suicidal drive into an idiopathic pain works to occlude, for example, Woolf's experience of sexual abuse at the hands of male relatives. As another poem here – about yet another woman coming to an unpleasant end – says, 'her torso blacked out, flat and simple like a stencil'.

Unlikely that Pajak takes as much aesthetic delight in specifically female suffering as this suggests, but his lack of intervention in his own – admittedly powerful – image-making leaves everything on the table. The greatest strength of *Slide* is therefore that which also opens the door to its greatest failings.

Satisfying the Ape

Don Paterson, *The Arctic* (Faber) £14.99
Reviewed by Hugh Foley

Don Paterson has had things figured out for a while now. In *The Arctic*, his seventh collection of original poems, if you manage to fiddle with the zoom on your phone camera, you'll find in the tiny-font concrete poem, 'Dot', a self-ironisingly technical-sounding philosophical statement on the 'arrogation of extrinsic purpose' by 'mind', and the future of machine consciousness which fits quite neatly into the kinds of things he says in his formidable 2018 treatise, *The Poem*. But really, the pith of his system seems to be pretty much the same as it was when he wrote *Nil Nil*: the universe is indifferent and cold. Death gives structure to time and our experience. 'Meaning' in the universe is a kind of delusion borne of our pattern-making ape brains. Even acts of interpersonal miscommunication repeat the pattern of desperate, death-denying pattern seeking. Poems exploit our urge to find a source of meaning outside of ourselves, and for this reason should be tightly patterned, orderly things from which the bottom drops out, an ultimately arbitrary way of satisfying the ape while giving you a glimpse of the real, profound nothingness.

By now, Paterson's cold, indifferent universe is familiar enough to feel cosy. *The Arctic* takes its title from a bar in Dundee where the speaker of 'The Alexandrian Library', his ongoing mini-epic, hangs out to await the end of the world by nuclear holocaust. It's a good joke; the arctic is a nice warm stand-in for the Patersonian absolute zero.

And so the new book continues as he means to end. In the opener, 'Repertoire', a sonnet elegising his father, Paterson refuses to 'curate / for their piquancy' the titles of the last songs his father, who suffered from dementia, remembered how to play. Instead of picking more meaningful songs, he rhymes the uncooperatively prosaic titles with the word 'true': '"Truck Driving Man" and "Good Old Mountain Dew"'. Rhyme has always been Paterson's go-to guardrail for his guided tours of the abyss. It's a trick he likely picked up from Paul Muldoon, but which he has stripped back to impressive effect in a number of poems, including this one.

The elegies for Paterson's father are among the book's best. In 'Snaba', the poet comes to understand the 'meaning' of his father's nickname for him on the latter's deathbed: 'Snowball', in Scots. In a way, the metaphor implicit in the nickname becomes apt, finally, as Paterson sees himself moving closer to death as he gets closer to his father:

> And now the boy
> with the white hair and the white beard holds
> his knees and makes himself very small and round
> because now he is very cold and he has no father.

This is lovely, and, of course, both arbitrary and temporary, a momentary stay not against but within confusion.

Ploughing through *The Arctic*, however, one hits quite a few obstacles. Readers will have to establish their own level of tolerance for the inevitable Patersonian *jeux d'esprit*, including the concrete poem, but also aphorisms, jokes about 'Women in 80s Movies', etc. The best of the banter poems is an address 'To his Penis' in Scots. Like some of the other poems, it's implicitly asking 'are you triggered, you censorious young puritans'. But it's charming and harmless enough.

More unforgivably turgid is the political writing. There should be a rule that this kind of stuff has to be at least as funny as newspaper sketch writers – a low bar that Paterson cracks his shins on repeatedly. 'Spring Letter' is probably the worst poem Paterson has written. Charitably put, it's a discussion of our impotence as observers of both political spectacle and the real horrors of the Russian invasion of Ukraine alike. But it's disastrously high on its own supply of zingers. If calling (presumably) Dominic Cummings 'Wormtongue' or Boris Johnson 'bin-fire Churchill' calms you down while watching the news, fair enough, but slack self-satisfaction swallows up the outrage and resignation. Still, the real problem comes when you get the feeling that Paterson is being serious, and not just trying to sound like a versified John Crace:

> Personally I blame it all on God
> or at least the human tendency to place
> whoever in the gang's most like a god
> at the centre of the party, class, team, office
> and use their psychopathic certainty

to act as we would not dare otherwise...

I'd wager that 'the human tendency' to look for certainties explains nothing about geopolitics or Russian militarism. But this easy certainty about the dangers of certainty is a feature, not a bug. It's what his poems emerge from. Even when he's writing brilliantly, Paterson's absent god, his big zero, is too big. Everything fits inside it, but it comes out looking the same. Divide by zero and you get to infinity, too easily.

Even at this book's best, Paterson is too in control of his material. It offers only a token resistance to his technical skill and philosophical artillery. We are always in the presence of a man who knows that no one makes it out alive. And so they don't.

Words about Words about Words

Anne Stevenson, *Collected Poems* (Bloodaxe) £25
Reviewed by Chris McCully

This is a scrupulously-prepared and – at over 560 pages, spanning well over twenty works published between 1965 and 2020 – a generous *Collected Poems*. Notionally, the works assembled here range chronologically from *Living in America* (1965) – a volume showing the impress of the demotic precision of Elizabeth Bishop – to *Completing the Circle* (2020). It's impossible to be accurate about the number of collections included here because Stevenson was an inveterate reviser and set new or reworked pieces within, for example, a previous *Collected*, which included work written and published from 1955–95.

Often called an 'Anglo-American poet', Stevenson stated candidly that if she belonged anywhere, it was to places and countries – a particular kind of America, possibly another kind of England or Wales – which no longer existed: that sense of transience and passage is explored not in sentimental wistfulness but in an often robust, outwardly-directed form of awareness (birds, stone walls, gestures, discarded dresses, formerly smoke-filled pub rooms... Like Hardy, she noticed such things). Assembled here is almost sixty years' worth of making, inheriting and inhabiting poetry:

> And why inhabit, make, inherit poetry?
> Oh, it's the shared comedy of the worst
> blessed; the sound leading the hand;
> a wordlife running from mind to mind
> through the washed rooms of the simple senses;
> one of those haunted, undefendable, unpoetic
> crosses we have to find.
> (from 'Making Poetry', 1985)

I should declare an interest. Over forty years ago, when she held a Northern Arts Literary Fellowship, Anne Stevenson was one of my tutors at the University of Newcastle-upon-Tyne. Thereafter she became a lifelong correspondent. We didn't write or meet frequently and when we did, it was always on unequal terms: I never lost the feeling of being her star-struck student. Anne's correspondence was also characteristically generous, punctuated by invitations to stay at her beloved Pwllymarch (her home in Wales), just as her Christmas cards were always accompanied by a slip of paper on which she'd printed a new, and usually topical, poem.

Anne wasn't uncritical of others' works or lives but she was always sympathetic. Working through this *Collected*, what impressed me was that constant reiteration of shared solidarity, manifested often in outward-lookingness:

> Let me not live, ever, without pub people,
> the tattooed forearm steering the cue like a pencil,
> the twelve-pint belly who adds up the scores in his
> head,
> the wiry owner of whippets, the keeper of ferrets,
> thin wives who suffer, who are silent, who talk with
> their eyes...
> (from 'A Prayer to Live with Real People', 1985)

Over the years, that sense of kinship did darken into a form of recognition that was sometimes disconcerted or even appalled – 'There are too many of us', she writes in '17.14 out of Newcastle' (2004) or again, in 'Dover Beach Reconsidered', 'The tide withdraws and leaves us on a strand / Streaming with losses, shards, shells, stinking places' (2020) – but Anne never lost her sense of comradeship with her neighbours, particularly when those neighbours included fellow writers, those souls William Dunbar called *makars*. In *A Lament for the Makars* (2007), Stevenson revisits and calibrates her imaginative relationships with writers ranging from William Langland to Bishop and Sylvia Plath. Cast in a Dantean form of dialogues and overhearings, 'A Lament' finally celebrates 'the mind's harmonic mappings, / frail as gossamer, / *costing not less than everything*' and concludes on a note of wry resilience whose irony is entirely characteristic:

> I am alive. I'm human.
> Get dressed. Make coffee.
> Shore a few lines against my ruin.

Although she wrote often about other poets and writers and even produced two splendid, or splendidly controversial, works analysing the gifts of both Bishop and Plath, Anne was impatient with poetry that became too self-referential – 'Professional poems in incomprehensible argot... Words about words about words'. In her work and thinking there was always that difficult, necessary relationship with a troubled world to explore. She also, if gently, insisted that poems should be well-made and, through successive revisions, acquire sufficient precision to succeed in their own terms of reciprocal reason and feeling:

> I can't like poems that purposely muddy the waters,
> Confuse in order to impress...
>
> I wince at poems whose lazy prosodical morals
> Beget illegitimate rhymes....
>
> I wave off turbulent poems where reason and feeling
> Stand off like water and oil...
>
> Professional poems in incomprehensible argot
> Unsettle me more and more...
> (from 'An Old Poet's View from the Departure Platform', 2020)

In this insistence, Stevenson reminds me strongly of Yeats and, like Yeats claiming that his glory was borrowed from the power of his friends, one theme developed throughout Anne's work memorialises and thereby reifies the creative gifts of others, whether these are mothers, family members, friends, other writers or – particularly – musicians. Stevenson must be one of the greatest memorialists of the present century. Mozart, Beethoven and many other composers are remembered here, but so too are those who interpreted them: a memorial to the pianist Bernard Roberts –

> His spirit could be part of his piano.
> Playing it, arms crossed like Brahms,
> he guides his listening hands about the keys...
> (from 'Improvisation', 2020)

as well as a tribute to John Eliot Gardiner, conducting Beethoven in 2016:

> Flawless, repeatable, conscientiously *a tempo* –
> Beethoven, locked in his deafness,
> never dreamed for the march of his scherzo
> anything as wonderful as this...
> (from 'A Compensation of Sorts', 2020)

If I may speak for a moment as Anne's former student, then for Anne, evincing formal control of any poem was a prerequisite of convincing, competent writing: she expected any writer to be aware of and to use all the possibilities of their medium. I don't mean that Anne obliged her students to write in rhymed, metrical forms (though such an obligation may have done us good) but that she was more than usually aware of the freedom and the possibilities allowed by experiments with form. Anne's training as a musician – she studied both piano and cello – means that her poetry returns sometimes, always in significant ways, not only to musical themes but that a sense of phrasing invariably co-operates interestingly with Anne's control of the poetic line itself. This can be exemplified on every page of this *Collected*, but one instance will clarify what I mean. In the following, from a poem I've already cited, the line-internal phrasing is carefully patterned such that almost every line spans two syntactic phrases, whose boundary is symbolised by ...] [... in the examples following. That pattern is made explicit in the antepenultimate line of each of the three stanzas comprising the poem: 'O Russian dolls], [O range of hills...' or 'O zebra blouse,] [O vampish back...'. In the second stanza of the poem, that pattern breaks (into three phrases) at a significant thematic moment ('thin wives who suffer,] [who are silent,] [who talk with their eyes....') and a similar disruption can be found in the final line of the piece, which again breaks into three syntactic portions (note the carefully-placed comma after 'Habitat'). This emphasises a key theme of the poem – the distinction, or the lack of distinction, between life and literature:

> '... save me from Habitat,] [and snobbery] [and too damn much literary ambition.'
> (from 'A Prayer to Live with Real People')

One can't teach this subtle, well-gauged handling of a poetic line. It's something innate, some hyper-alertness to the harmonics of a mind in motion.

I'm grateful not only that Anne Stevenson was my teacher but that her poems – such precision and compassion, such aghast comprehension, over such a long span of time – have been finally collected into such a wonderful volume. This text should not only adorn a bookshelf; the contents of the work also show that in the end, 'art has to triumph over experience' and thereby provide readers and listeners with equipment vital for endurance in what Stevenson called a 'terrifying century'.

Still Slugging Back the Red

Hannah Sullivan, *Was It for This* (Faber) £12.99
Reviewed by Daisy Fried

Like her picaresque and dazzling debut *Three Poems*, Hannah Sullivan's follow-up comprises three long poem sequences that showcase her virtuoso image-making, rangy scene setting, and casually impeccable ear. *Three Poems* focused on three cities where Sullivan has lived; *Was It for This*, also quite urban, concerns itself with homes – buying and selling them, as places of origin and places we leave; pleasurable places that shape us, places we lose; places of constraint, of safety that turns out not to be safe. In verse lines and in prose paragraphs, Sullivan employs prismatic shifts in focus and vantage, but her voice, whatever that is, is unmistakable throughout. Lots of motherhood, some Covid lockdown, lots of wanders into the past, some whiffs of a terrifying present. This time: less youthful ennui, more midlife retrospection.

And Sullivan now observes other people's suffering, especially that of the victims of the 2017 Grenfell Tower fire. On one hand, this deepens things, as the poet considers the ways the personal is – and also isn't – a way in to other people's experience. This also risks creating the kinds of problems that artists encounter when writing as witness rather than as survivor. But Sullivan's solutions – even when imperfect– are interesting and ethical.

The Grenfell Tower disaster began with an electrical fire in a tenant's refrigerator ('It would have crumbled under water jets', writes Sullivan in 'Tenants', the book's first poem) and spread with ferocious speed because of deficient regulation and developer non-compliance with safety regulations. The victims were overwhelmingly immigrants, asylum seekers, poor working class, and many died because emergency operators directed them to shelter in place instead of evacuating. 'Tenants' moves between the West Kensington fire and Sullivan's first-person accounts – in, I think, deliberately flat, numb blank verse – of caring for a baby in a nearby posh neighbourhood:

> On dry grey days we went to Holland Park.
> The little children's playground was revamped.
> It cost a million pounds and looked the same.
> [...]
> The baby on my lap, for safety sniffing him,
> Addicted to his warm, sweet yeasty smell
> [...]
> I was absconding from the life that I had had...

What stance might such a poet-speaker take towards the horror a few blocks over? Sullivan thankfully doesn't perform outrage or focus on her own feelings. Out and about with the pram, she buys eczema cream, 'Making my hands flat, flammable, the residues on clothes'. An uncomfortable move, to place quotidian maternal anxiety about fire safety close by mothers dying in their flats. Sullivan knows this, and has conditioned us from the beginning of the poem to deal with moves between terror and complacency. 'Tenants' opens historically with a blitzkrieg bomb ('silver pencil in the sky'), segues to a more recent past in which old women watch 'the renovation of the tower, / Built in the emptiness the bomb had cleared', to a set piece about a beehive collapse – image analogous to a burnt-out apartment? – thence to pan the neighbourhood, and baby care in Holland Park.

Dispassionate description is, in poetry of witness, a means of marking, but avoiding appropriating, trauma. Journalism documents and disseminates that sort of thing better, on the whole, than poems do, however; poets in that mode can seem opportunistic, in search of a topic because they're poets, rather than writing what's necessary. Sullivan's work here is good, deriving acts of the imagination from materials from an official Grenfell Tower inquiry:

> The man who planned to tie his daughter to his chest,
> Step into air, flip up,
> Go lying on his back to break her fall.
> And on the way that baby was delivered,
> The silence as they dressed him this one time

Sullivan's pacing and prosody here is perfect, her pentameter line lengthened like a pause before a leap, then the eerie quick float in the shortened line when the man steps and flips, then the return to pentameter with impact, to terrible news of another mother's baby delivered through inference rather than direct explanation. That moment, where the reader has to make a leap to understand, invites honest feeling. It matters too that Sullivan drastically breaks prosody, adapting what appears to be transcripts of emergency calls, but staying otherwise out of the way of ghosts:

The fire brigade are coming	Can you be quick look Please?
I said they're on the way OK?	
You only called just now	I said it's jumping up
Look	Look!
	It's going up and over
I said you need to stay	and it's going down
It's only ten past one	Hello?
	Hello?

In the book's next, title, poem, Sullivan's homes are places to live and real estate. Grenfell echoes here too in 1965 testimony from the Grenfell architect regarding the tower's planning and safety prior to its construction. This connects poem to poem in a book of diverse means and ambitions. 'Was It for This', the poem, employs prose as well as verse. The prose tends to register as anecdotal – a whiff of notebooks written towards, but not yet achieving, art (this serves the poem). Sullivan's verse lines burrow into experience via complex syntax and other poetic stunts. By contrast, Sullivan's prose, well, chills out.

This can feel desultory. I don't mind reading, but am not sure why I need to, a memory of prank calls to a teacher – but when the same teacher eats 'a kiwi fruit with a spoon, as if it were a boiled egg', I snap to attention – such a good image. 'The absence of coherence', wrote Leon Wieseltier, 'is not yet incoherence'; Sullivan's virtue here is that, in her divided modal ambitions – towards reportage, personal narrative, diary, lyric epiphany – she never attempts, but rather resists, synthesis.

It's not merely anecdotal: when she recounts house-hunting pregnant, 'easy prey' in her maternity dress for realtors, Sullivan shifts vantage soon after to other stressed-out women 'who smoked in the kitchen or left the unchanged litter tray out, determined to obstruct and delay the sale for as long as possible'. She also recalls her own stint working in real estate selling a crummy flat ('the metal casements looked as if they'd been eroded with acid') to a man because it was 'very cheap, and he was divorcing'. He fixes up the place, and when 'the front door was painted, and blinds went up on the lidless windows, it gave me', Sullivan writes, 'a feeling of calm and restitutive rightness'.

Who gets restitution, calm, rightness? Does it last? The book's final poem, 'Happy Birthday', marks the poet-speaker's forty-first, and continues the *mezzo cammin* mood (elsewhere Sullivan quotes Dante outright on getting *smarrita* – as it seems all poets must on reaching a certain age). Plenty of zeitgeist: 'my friends all / 40+, harassed by infants, joylessly / still slugging back the red'.

I'll read that to my wine-mom pals, harassed by teens, at our next gathering. Life contains plenty of amusing filler, and so does this poem, as when the poet googles trivia related to the number forty-one (dial code of Switzerland, number of Mozart's symphonies, unlucky number in Japan, age at death of Alan Turing and Jane Austen). But Sullivan moves into another list, of events on the day of her 1979 birth, including 'a woman paralysed by polio / … burnt to death', and this connects glancingly back to 'Tenants', while apprehending the simultaneity of disparate human experiences. Networks of reference: this is signature Sullivan. And all that discursion keeps on elaborating itself. You might think, towards the end of 'Happy Birthday', that we're meandering again, this time a river tubing excursion, where a cooler of 'high-hopped session ales', strapped into its own tube, goes 'a little pompously…' astray.

We found it on a sandbar
where a man was grilling fruit…
[…]
I tried to grab your dinghy back
he said – and then broke off,
his open palm extended
vaguely, speckled with cilantro.

But then the man gestures again, and detail becomes image becomes epiphany:

towards the estuary where
smolt adapt to saltwater,
go silvery and shoal
and later will return
full-grown to spawn.

This would make a pretty-ravishing traditional standalone lyric in another poet's book, as a bit of sport and beer become an urge to home and spawn. But restitution – resolution – doesn't stick here either. The river of the poem flows on. New section. Poet calls to kids. Mom gives poet advice about killing moths. A coat is 'eaten out' (sexy echoes?) by moths. Things crumble, syntax gets knotty, because – I think – life is knotty, and crumbly, and the poem ends not with epiphany's resolving glow, but in standoff, 'the flashiness of staring down / tomorrow'.

Truth & Beauty

Harry Clifton, *Gone Self Storm* (Bloodaxe) £10.99
Lavinia Singer, *Artifice* (Prototype) £12.00
Reviewed by Tara Bergin

I received my review copies of these two new books back in March, just before the long weekend of St. Patrick's Day and Mothering Sunday. It seemed an unusual combination of holidays; one which, according to the woman in the off-license that Saturday, proved very bad for the sale of fine wines. 'You don't taste the good wine properly if you glug it back', she said to me (a little accusatorily); 'you have to hold it in your mouth for ages and squash it through your teeth.' 'Yes', I said, as if I knew. I was in fact grateful for the image, because it struck me as an excellent way to think about reading these two new poetry collections, both of which I feel also deserve to be savoured.

I'll start with *Gone Self Storm*, by the distinguished Irish poet Harry Clifton. On the one hand, the poems in this new collection are very personal; the lyric 'I' and 'eye' are dominant. The book opens pre-birth – at the moment of conception – and closes pre-death – contemplation of the end. The poems in between reflect on journeys and homecomings, on the passing of friends and loved ones, and on the position of the writer, watching the world, 'with the eye of a stepchild'.

On the other hand the poems move beyond the personal, exploring and questioning the human experiences of discovery, aging and loss. It is a book of innocence and experience, but even the poems of innocence – birth, childhood, and youth – are informed by a mood of probability and knowing; a 'language of conditionals, subjunctives / In a land of might-have-been'.

The wisdom is felt in terms of craft too. Harry Clifton handles his material deftly; he keeps a firm hold on both content and form. The subtle rigour of these poems is immediately evident: capital letters at the start of every line (they come 'dressed for dinner' as John Clegg would say); stanzas, couplets; quatrains. Linger longer (hold the wine in your mouth) and you discover a perceptive use of pace and music; it runs throughout the collection – for example in 'Toome' towards the end of the book:

Poor in everything
But water. Unconsecrated,
Not yet changed to wine,
I made it mine,

Where time condenses
Into years

And a heartspace clears
Between nothing and nothing.

Such poems are made for the mouth and the breath; they are a joy to read aloud, and doing so increases the pleasure and understanding. This is not due to an overt theatricality, but more to a delicate balancing of ease and restriction; an ability to 'dip the visual into the self', as Marina Tsvetaeva put it, and vice versa, while maintaining the artistic distance required for drafting and shaping. These poems combine the spoken and the written word with ease and elegance.

The book's title is taken from a note that Keats scribbled in the margin of a book in 1817. In it emotions are compared to wine, and the poet to someone who 'by one cup should know the scope of any particular wine without getting intoxicated'. The woman in the off-license would approve of that. The next step for a poet, summarises Keats, is to 'paint from memory of gone self storms'.

I suspect that Harry Clifton's choice of this phrase for his title hints at both his subject ('the man that suffers') and his method ('the mind that creates'). There is a lesson in it: poems are made things. See 'The Felling', a poem in five parts that describes the cutting down of a group of pine trees. A smell of resin still remains in the grove, and there are growth rings in the logs left over: 'Circles within circles, closed, / Inscrutable now, whatever their wisdom was'.

When the speaker of the poem puts one of the logs on the fire, he hears the wind, but 'without the trees'. It is an image that manages to convey not only the specific moment in the poet's memory, but also the haunting (and haunted) act of making poems.

*

Lavinia Singer's debut collection *Artifice* (the word literally means 'art make') takes the idea of poem-as-made-thing into a visually playful realm. This collection brings us the other extreme of contemporary poetry: fragmentation; experimentation; the poem as object. Even the cover image alerts us to its conscious blend of contemporary poetics and traditional craftwork: the title is placed at the very top of the cover, its letters decorated in a manner reminiscent of a beautiful medieval manuscript. Beneath it is a large blank space, and then the poet's name in block caps, right at the foot of the page. This is the aesthetic of the notebook; very appealing to handle and to hold, and it looks great lying on the table. These things are not merely superficial. In one interview Lavinia Singer talked about her love of the artist's notebook and the 'pleasure of touching, holding and owning'.

The poems make inventive use of typography – gaps, over-lappings, dashes, crossings-out, little flower motifs, like this:

The presentation is superb: Protoype, the forward-thinking London-based publisher, aims to make books that are beautiful and unique. With this in mind it makes sense that the first poem of the book, called 'Work Study', is inspired by an artist's studio. It sets the tone in its celebration of the loveliness of stuff: 'The brush pots, clippings, tinted tea mugs and dead colour worked into wall creases'. It's out of all this 'junk', concludes the poem, that 'the Work' is made.

Codes, found text, ekphrasis, truncated sentences and shaped poems follow. What they 'mean' or what they are 'about' is not always easy to know on a first reading. 'Compass Rose' for example, is a poem typed in two directions and making the shape of a cross, with the centre, overlapping text rendered indecipherable. The outer edges suggest outlooks or viewpoints, but are so fragmented so that it's hard to be sure. Here, for example, is the upper section labelled 'N' for North:

left of the rising sun
winter winds wake and
on my garden blow old
air phlegmatic boreas
aquilo seven oxen at
the plough bearded
man an arctic night

It is sensation, not narrative, that drives this poem at first encounter and many of the pieces present their argument in this way: with suggestions and absences.

In others, the story is more readily graspable, but even these take a sidelong approach, often drawing on research and study to imagine another world, another voice, another time – yet these are worlds, voices, times which prove strikingly parallel to our own. See for example 'The Mapmaker's Daughter', where the loss of forests is depicted through the work of a cartographer whose maps gradually change in colour from the greens of trees to the blues of water: 'Now all Dad needs is tins of cyan, / turquoise and teal and ultramarine, / the blues of midnight, lavender and sky'. It's an impressively effective way of talking about climate change.

The poem ends with the daughter looking at her father's old Ordnance Survey. It sums everything up with a devastating simplicity, showing: 'a world I can barely believe. / A world that was marvellous, that was good.'

A Vortex of Violence

Bhanu Kapil, *Incubation: a space for monsters* (Prototype) £12
Reviewed by Jazmine Linklater

It feels almost redundant to attempt a logical review of a text so committed to nonlinearity. *Incubation* is a necessarily fragmented and chaotic experience. Look the book up online and you repeatedly see three categorisations: 'Poetry. Cross Genre. Asian American Studies'. OK. I have seen Kapil, rightly, reviewed alongside Claudia Rankine, and other contemporary genre-defiant poets spring to mind: Monica Youn and Layli Long Soldier, for example. *Incubation* is rangy and deviant. It's about otheredness, roaming around the outsides of anything static. Most Goodreads reviews are awe-struck, poetic responses to the embodied experience of reading the text. My favourite, a two-star review, reads: 'it helps to read it as poetry rather than as a novel. Because it's not a novel. Just a bunch of words in prose form.' Yes. Readers found it 'beautiful', 'confusing', 'mesmerising'. Yes.

The distinct tone and character of the work emerges from the constant conflation of its parts: anecdotes/memories/diary entries delivered by a narrator/lyric speaker who is sometimes the protagonist, Laloo, who is also you, the reader, and Kapil the writer, the girl, monster, cyborg, immigrant, mother, other. Yes, this book is composed of lists, both sequential and jumbled. It's always about both. 'I wanted to write opposites', she repeats. It is always she, except when it's He (patriarchal): father, baker, butcher, driver of the car she gets into while hitchhiking in 'the land of known mutilators'. The text repeatedly invokes dyads while sticking two fingers up at the logic of binary opposition. Indeed my British edition of *Incubation* is a 'non-identical variant' of the US edition, each newly expanded with their own coda (it is always about appendages). These two new editions are themselves non-identical variants of the original 2006 edition, possibly reworked in additional ways.

A young brown British girl flees the country of her birth to hitchhike around America, while refusing a masculinised literary urge towards linearity. In place of Kerouac's scroll, Laloo is 'tearing out the pages as I go', submerging them, drying them out, rearranging them. The logbook she keeps is not the shipmaster's, noting the date and weather, but a mess of experiences, emotions, garbled memory overlaying itself. Certainly time is important, in its multiplicity. Timelines are not quite parallel but bump up against one another unexpectedly, overlapping both in the material production of these reissued texts and their stories. *Incubation* is like a bildungsroman: Laloo's girlhood morphs into adulthood; Kapil returns to England and reissues a formative part of her body of work. We return to a beginning, replete with shades of Kapil's later work. Laloo flees the British white nationalism that Ban will later unpack while lying on the ground in *Ban en Banlieue*; she begins to articulate the diasporic trauma that *Schizophrene* will more explicitly unpack; she is repeatedly thwarted by the vicious host logic which is distilled in her most publicly celebrated book, *How To Wash a Heart*.

Here it is all viscerally embodied. Laloo is sexed, her awareness increasing, becoming desirous and encountering 'risk, as a kind of twin to permission' in a fantasy of freedom that hitchhikes, writes, fornicates. She is always menstruating ('Laloo means red'), navigating the learnt shame, navigating the variable levels of agency she can permit herself. Sometimes, succumbing to sex is the safest option – the only way to get out alive. And sex sometimes leads to pregnancy, but Laloo is always pregnant ('at age nine'), always born her/himself 'appended by a parasite' and displayed as a circus freak around the US.

The pregnancy metaphor, explicitly figured as parasitical, necessarily includes its attendant moment of birthing. Severing, splitting one into two, is the making of mothers. The motherland. 'This is blood text' about borders, inheritance, memory and trauma: it's about Partition, latently. 'The removal of a person, abruptly, from a set of conditions, is complicated for the soul.' It's about how what is separated is never removed, even when 'our babies are taken away by a customer or nurse standing in line': care must continue to be cultivated. But everything costs money here, 'the patient is always a client'. Because the healthcare settings in which these births take place are always instruments of oppressive surveillance by the nation state: even when nativity creates nationality it can still be denied. Laloo gives us her alien number, her national security number, even her phone number. She interfaces with the Department of Homeland Security in search of 'temporary-permanent' status. She is a second-generation immigrant who flees to become an immigrant who gives birth to an ambiguously second-generation immigrant. So she fantasises repeatedly about a 'fake country' where its infrastructures don't all conspire against her, where she has the freedom to write, or to hitchhike less fugitively.

Because going – hitchhiking – isn't escaping. *Incubation* recreates a vortex of violence that implicates everyone, domestically and globally. White supremacy coexists with Hindutva nationalism. In childhood, asking her mother about angels: 'she hit me, because we were Hindus'. Generational trauma is passed down in surreally grotesque scenes as when, preparing their father's meal, her sisters work 'through occasional bouts of intense abdominal pain', menstruating and miscarrying: a 'discharge of bones with what was coming out already'. Child Laloo scrubs the 'wet place' on the floor where she saw the aborted 'human hand, no bigger than a grape, crumpled up yet obviously that'. Elsewhere violence is perpetrated by characters' ignorance about the histories of empire ('Are you from India? [...] I bet they don't have scones over there, do they?') and the ongoing coloniality of contemporary nation states (at the border: 'scone and jam emporiums and holding centres'). Kapil never forgets that humour can aid the absorption of horror.

And despite all this, or because of it, assimilation is often her goal, more often her 'monstrous' failure. She concedes: 'I cannot go further west than this'. So *Incubation* now, in this new edition, is about return: returning to Britain to revise, redouble and recreate. Is the 'Handwritten Preface to Reverse the Book' new, written in 2023 with one eye on 2006? You could read it as such. But *Incubation* is about acknowledging the past and holding it up without rewriting it. The new coda proposes an alternative epigraph whilst letting the original stand: enacting both as distinct but entangled possibilities. Carrying history while it feeds on our bones. Where *How to Wash a Heart* clarified part of Kapil's overarching project, this return complicates it again – makes a mess of 'the larger sense of a bodily organisation: its complex workings and ways of communicating across systems'. It feels to me like a more enquiring articulation of what it's like to live in, amongst, under the oppressive political structures we inhabit. It feels more confusing, more dangerous, more sexy and funny and unbearable, which is what makes it good art, because it feels like life.

Broken Statues

Yannis Ritsos, *Monochords* (Prototype) £15
Reviewed by Rowland Bagnall

One of the most prominent Greek poets of the twentieth century, Yannis Ritsos (1909–90) was exiled to Samos in the late 1970s. Under house arrest during the summer of 1979, he composed a sparse sequence of 336 one-line poems, combining diaristic observations with evocative reflections. Enigmatic and fragmentary, *Monochords* stands both as an interior and exterior archive, 'a surrealist calendar', writes Thurston Moore, measuring the passing days, 'seeking hope in the real'. Translated by Paul Merchant with quiet authority, Prototype presents the sequence with linocuts by Chiara Ambrosio, who responded to the poems through a period of lockdown.

Written over a month (an average rate of ten per day), the monochords pick out minor details: 'A long Sunday with cypresses, with birds and water jars', 'Each moment a tree, a bird, a smokestack, a woman'. They aim for 'The physical *fact* of things and situations', writes Gareth Evans, a quality of truthfulness, mining for the essence of experience and landscape. Ritsos captures a world of 'Things that are themselves', to borrow a phrase from the poet Jack Gilbert, 'Waves water, the rocks / stone', discovering ingredients that we can be certain of: 'A white horse in a yellow field', 'a basket of tomatoes'.

These specks are sifted from a damaged environment; the Greece of Ritsos's poems bears traces of political and civil unrest, from handcuffs, soldiers and broken glass to 'rocks from a stoning', 'a drowned woman', even 'Corpses on the pavements'. 'I create lines to exorcise the evil that has oppressed my country', he writes, the poems both a witness and response to national turbulence. At the same time, they begin the slow work of repair, their language summoning the world anew, speaking it into existence: 'Sweet corn, grapes, a donkey, the sky'. Their sparseness compels us into a process of collaboration. The poems 'stir up a world', inviting us to flesh it out, drawing colour from our own lives, our experience and memories.

For all his observational precision, Ritsos also drifts into moments of oblique and cryptic meditation, hinting at 'The meaning outside meanings', encouraging interrogation. Ambrosio brings this quality of the poems out beautifully in her linocuts, in which objects, scenes and animals are tinged, slightly, with magic. Beside her prints, Ritsos's poems inherit the texture of Ovid's *Metamorphoses*, a world in which everyday trees and buildings, birds and pistachios, rub happily alongside supernatural transformations. 'A lemon on the bare table. It glows', suggests one poem; 'In the field I found Yesenin's cow observing a small cloud', reports another. This is a Samos of magical acts, 'as if a miracle were the most natural of things'.

The endless interplay of text and image here holds something of the emblematic. Indeed, as Lucy Mercer writes in *Emblem* (Prototype, 2022), her debut collection, the two constantly 'reinterpret and reinforce each other, inducing murky contemplation as we move from one part to another and back again'. David Harsent draws attention to the poems' interpretive potential in his introduction: the words and images may be simple, but 'there's always more to it than that'.

Ritsos attunes us to a double present, to the world as it happens and as we interpret it. Gareth Evans is right to point us to John Berger: 'to read a poem means to be transported [...] to a place where future and past fall away and there is only here and now', he writes, 'a here and now which sings and includes everything'. *Monochords* invites us in, acknowledging its constant passing, making each note all the more significant: 'You know? In a while it'll be over'.

Into Sight

Zoë Skoulding, *A Marginal Sea* (Carcanet) £11.99
Tom French, *Company* (Gallery Press) £12.95
Reviewed by Bebe Ashley

In Zoë Skoulding's *A Marginal Sea,* there is some comfort to be found in reminding ourselves 'we are where we are' ('A Short Presentation on the Current Direction of Travel') while dreaming of a world slightly further away, or out of reach, from the coastal vantage point much of the book is written from, Ynys Môn. Recently shortlisted for the 2023 Wales Poetry Book of the Year Award, *A Marginal Sea*, with its vibrancy of language, transports readers to new perspectives: 'the grip of morning / never lets you down / carries you into / high wires of pines / their vertical tang' (Red Squirrels in Coed Cyrnol) where even the things in the shadows or 'beyond the island's lunar edges' are drawn into sight.

Perspective is a fundamental aspect of play throughout Skoulding's work. In 'Gullscape', a poem which takes its title from a painting by Roy Lichtenstein, Skoulding asks, 'HOW FAR CAN YOU SEE / from the same place / daily wheeling / around the town'. There is humour here, in how long an inanimate object like a painting can show you the same view, but sadness too, in how quickly monotony and routine overshadow the things on the periphery and the just beyond.

Tangible landscapes are beautifully created at height but further excel at sea level: 'feet slide on sand and small roots / off the edge of a map where land is / churned to wave form under wind' ('Newborough Warren with Map of Havana'), as light and sound give way to texture that feels lush and lyrical: 'under oily shimmer / soundings from space / stars a wilderness flashed / off the surface' ('A Strait Story').

A Marginal Sea is very nearly bookended by conversations in which animals and the environment are given equal weight as conversation partners capable of reply. However, our role as humans intervening in a natural world is acknowledged throughout, sometimes highlighting moments of absurdity. Looking for the grave of Rosa Luxemburg in 'A Rose for Rosa', Skoulding's confident switch in form entertains the role of the geographic legacy of naming: 'she is not in the jardins rosa luxemburg in paris or the jardins de rose luxemburg in barcelona where although you may find roses you will not find her'.

If Rosa Luxembourg is difficult to locate, other aspects of the contemporary world drift into view of the poems easily. With a closing mention of microplastics, Skoulding's questioning of modernity and the richness of a life rooted to one place is threaded closed, ensuring that this is a collection that will be turned to again and again. 'Had this been life? So much / glitter and strip light so much / money and love / yes call it that' ('During the Works').

Tom French's seventh collection, and winner of the 2023 Pigott Prize, *Company* demonstrates confidence in its use of artistic and historic sources to explore and interrogate the sense of place and the role of humanity within that place. Alongside *A Marginal Sea*, *Company* drew the interest of judging panels in being a collection that celebrates the variety of rural communities: 'You're not the first stranger. Come now again' with the more often than not harsh environmental realities you can expect there, 'Tonight's fire's lit. Their bones are berthed / in the last dry ground before ground gives out. This threshold holds against the very tide. / Call here a port. Call all outdoors a storm' ('Agnes Moran's, Mornington').

Rarely does a title in French's collection not reference a time, place or artwork if not referencing all three at once as in 'Still Life, Chancellorsville, May 1863' or 'Michael Landy's *Break Down* (2001)'; readers will have an extensive list of source material to explore alongside the work.

In this coordinating framework, poems are best when personalities are richly replicated on the page: 'A voice from the body of the church requests / on behalf of all of the others and itself / that a chord not be held for absolutely ages', ('Áine O'Dwyer's Music for Church Cleaners Vols I and II'). This movement across time and geographic and metaphoric space is sometimes disconcerting: a turn of the page can take you leaping from the nineteenth to the twenty-first century then back again to the twentieth. The use of third person pronouns here also amplifies, to its detriment, this distance between the poet and the speaker of the poem. Poems that should linger with the reader in their challenging subject matter such as 'Commission' – 'One was hugging her teddy and sucking / her thumb the night she delivered her son' – seem diluted in their impact as the significant number of characters and speakers added to the collection give little time for readers to be convinced of each poem's speaker holding a unique, or memorable, tone.

Of the many poems now emerging about, and written in, the pandemic, French closes *Company* with two divergent approaches to sharing his personal experiences. *To Distance* is a lengthy sequence beginning with three epigraphs, perhaps replicating the overwhelm of daily information. The simpler images detailing the actions of the individual are strongest here: 'While we waited for restrictions to ease / we will be able to say we planted trees'.

This is followed by 'The Last Day', a more restrained three-stanza poem that marks the moment of moving onwards from the time we've held each other at a distance with a reminder of our inevitable and longed for closeness: 'It was the last day of February and minus one, / the last day of the longest winter we've known, / and it took days for it not to feel like history / to be seeing faces and taking a deep breath, / and not to think of distance when we met'.

Some Contributors

Duncan MacKay is a Senior Research Fellow at the Centre for Astrophysics & Planetary Science, University of Kent. He has published most recently with Muscaliet Press and Litmus Publishing. **Stav Poleg**'s debut poetry collection, *The City*, was published by Carcanet in Spring 2022. Her work has appeared in *The New Yorker* and *New Poetries VIII* (Carcanet, 2021), among others. **Tony Roberts** is the author of five collections of poetry and two books of essays on poets and critics for Shoestring Press, most recently *The Taste of My Mornings* (2019). He is currently completing a third. **Sam Adams** edited *Poetry Wales* in the early 1970s and has been a contributor to *PN Review* since 1982. **Jane Duran** was born in Cuba and raised in the USA and Chile. Selections of her poems have appeared in *Poetry Introduction 8* (Faber 1993), *Making for Planet Alice* (Bloodaxe 1997), and *Modern Women Poets* (Bloodaxe 2005). *The Clarity of Distant Things* was published by Carcanet in 2021. **Oksana Maksymchuk** is the author of the poetry collections *Xenia* and *Lovy* in the Ukrainian. Her English-language poems appeared in *AGNI*, *The Irish Times*, *The Paris Review*, *The Poetry Review* and other journals. With Max Rosochinsky she co-edited *Words for War: New Poems from Ukraine*, and co-translated *Apricots of Donbas* by Lyuba Yakimchuk and *The Voices of Babyn Yar* by Marianna Kiyanovska. **Silis MacLeod** is a retired librarian from the Isle of Harris. She is compiling a folk history of transhumance in the Scottish Highlands. **Joey Connolly** grew up in Sheffield, studied in Manchester and now works in London as the Director of Faber Academy. He received an Eric Gregory award in 2012, and his first collection, *Long Pass*, was published by Carcanet in 2017. *The Recycling* was published in 2023. **Jon Glover**'s poetry collections include *Glass is Elastic* (Carcanet, 2012). He co-edited (with Kathryn Jenner) Jon Silkin's *Complete Poetry* for Carcanet/Northern House. **Rory Waterman** is the author of three collections from Carcanet: the PBS Recommendation *Tonight the Summer's Over* (2013), shortlisted for the Seamus Heaney Award; *Sarajevo Roses* (2017), shortlisted for the Ledbury Forte Prize; and *Sweet Nothings* (2020). **Tom Pickard** grew up in the working-class suburbs of Cowgate, Newcastle upon Tyne, and Blakelaw, and left school at the age of fourteen. As a poet, Pickard is known for his range, from erotic to political, from lyrically delicate to poignantly sad to bluntly expletive-driven. As well as poetry Pickard has compiled books of oral history and has directed and produced a number of documentary films. **Jamie Osborn** is a poet, translator and activist, now in Norwich. His work is featured in Carcanet's *New Poetries VII*. **Mara-Daria Cojocaru** is a philosopher and poet from Germany, living in the UK. As a poet, she has published four books of poetry in German and has won numerous prizes (e.g. the German Prize for Nature Writing in 2021 or the Bavarian Young Talents Award for Literature in 2017). **Jazmine Linklater** is a poet and writer currently based in Manchester, UK. Her pamphlet, *Figure a Motion*, was published in September 2020 by Guillemot Press. **Sasha Dugdale** is a poet and translator. She has published five collections with Carcanet. *Deformations*, her most recent collection, was shortlisted for the 2020 T. S. Eliot and Derek Walcott Prizes. She has published numerous translations of Russian women's writing. The most recent of these, Maria Stepanova's novel *In Memory of Memory* (Fitzcarraldo, 2021), was shortlisted for the International Booker Prize. She is former editor of *Modern Poetry in Translation* and a Fellow of the Royal Society of Literature.

Editors
Michael Schmidt
John McAuliffe

Editorial Manager
Andrew Latimer

Contributing Editors
Anthony Vahni Capildeo
Sasha Dugdale
Will Harris

Copyeditor
Maren Meinhardt

Designed by
Andrew Latimer

Editorial address
The Editors at the address on the right. Manuscripts cannot be returned unless accompanied by a stamped addressed envelope or international reply coupon.

Trade distributors
NBN International

Represented by
Compass IPS Ltd

ISBN 978-1-80017-371-2
ISBN 0144-7076

Subscriptions—6 issues
INDIVIDUAL–print and digital: £45; abroad £65
INSTITUTIONS–print only: £76; abroad £90
INSTITUTIONS–digital only: from Exact Editions (https://shop.exacteditions.com/gb/pn-review)
to: PN Review, Alliance House, 30 Cross Street, Manchester, M2 7AQ, UK.

Supported by